THE BUSINESS OWNER'S GUIDE TO ACHIEVING FINANCIAL SUCCESS

David A. Duryee
Management Advisory Services,
A Division of Moss Adams

IRWIN
Professional Publishing

Burr Ridge, Illinois
New York, New York

Senior sponsoring editor:	Amy Hollands Gaber
Project editor:	Mary Conzachi
Production manager:	Ann Cassady
Cover designer:	Tim Kaage
Art manager:	Kim Meriwether
Compositor:	Alexander Graphics, Inc.
Typeface:	11/13 Palatino
Printer:	Book Press

Library of Congress Cataloging-in-Publication Data

Duryee, David A.
    The business owner's guide to achieving financial success / David A. Duryee.
        p.   cm.
    ISBN 0-7863-0228-3
    1. Business enterprises—Finance.   I. Title.
HG4026.D87   1994
658.15—dc20

94–9329

Printed in the United States of America
1 2 3 4 5 6 7 8 9 0 BP 1 0 9 8 7 6 5 4

To those of you who have the guts, determination, energy, and creativity to start and run your own business, this book is respectfully dedicated. I can only hope that it provides some meaningful assistance along the way to achieving financial success.

Preface

This book is intended for business owners or managers who would like to learn the basics of business finance. It will also benefit a variety of advisors to closely held businesses, including attorneys, accountants, bankers, consultants, and financial planners.

The goal throughout this book is to present financial management in practical and down-to-earth terms, to take financial concepts out of the classroom and apply them to the day-to-day operations of your business. This is a survival manual that explains the *basics* of business finance so you can manage your business effectively from a financial standpoint.

If you want to learn more, you might take some college level courses or read more advanced texts, but it is really not necessary. If you understand and apply what is in this book, it is all you will need to define, measure, and achieve financial success in your business.

If your business already has a good chief financial officer or controller, it is still desirable for you to have a grasp of at least a basic level of finance. Without it, meaningful communication between you and your financial officer will be difficult.

This is also true of communication between you and your banker. Probably 95 percent of all business owners arrive at the bank not knowing how much money they will ultimately need, how long they will need it, or how and when they will pay it back. From the banker's standpoint, these are important things to know. This book will explain how you can answer questions like these.

Chapter 1 discusses business life cycles. Businesses pass through several distinct phases, and financial conditions and requirements change accordingly. Chapter 2 is an overview of the financial analysis and planning process. It describes the three basic steps in the financial management process:

1. Historical analysis.
2. Long-range planning.
3. Short-range planning.

Chapter 3 begins the discussion of historical analysis and focuses on the balance sheet. It describes in detail what to look for and the key relationships of the balance sheet that measure the liquidity and safety of your business. Chapter 4 explains how to analyze the income statement. It describes the key relationships that measure profitability. Chapter 5 incorporates elements from both the balance sheet and the income statement and focuses on how to measure the operating performance of your business.

Chapter 6 defines and measures cash flow, a very important aspect of your business. You pay your bills, taxes, payroll, and bank loans with cash, not profits. Cash flow is where you live on a day-to-day basis. Is it always the same as profits? If not, why not? How much cash flow should you have? This chapter will help you answer these and many other questions about cash flow. Chapter 7 is a case study that explores the problems and solutions of one particular company.

Chapter 8 is an introduction to the planning process. It discusses the various aspects of your business that need to be a part of your business plan. This process starts with a consideration of the proper strategy to employ and then moves into the financial area. Establishing a proper long-term strategy for your business is an important exercise that should be done at least annually. The fact is, most business owners do not do a very good job of planning. "What's for lunch?" is as far as some look into the future. Much more needs to be done, and Chapter 8 outlines this process.

Chapter 9 begins the discussion of long-range financial planning and introduces the concept of sustainable growth rates, how fast the business can safely grow without getting into trouble. For most readers, this will be a new concept. The fact that you can literally "grow broke" doesn't seem right. Most people believe that the more sales and profits, the better. This is not necessarily true, and this chapter will explain why.

Chapter 10 describes how to project your income statement. This is the first financial statement that is projected, and it can be forecasted on a default basis or according to your best estimates for sales and expenses. Chapter 11 describes how to project your balance sheets. How much will you have in accounts receivable or inventory three years from now? How much money will you need to borrow from the bank, if any? This chapter will show you how to answer these questions. Chapter 12 completes the long-range financial process by projecting cash flow and the key financial ratios.

Chapter 13 describes the short-range planning process. Using the techniques discussed in this chapter, you will be able to determine your seasonal needs for cash. You may start the year with enough cash, and finish the year with enough cash, but in between your seasonal activities may lead to a substantial shortfall. Planning for this cash need is a separate and distinct exercise; it will be an important aspect of your negotiations with the bank.

Chapter 14 discusses how to manage your business for maximum profitability. The concept of fixed and variable costs is introduced in this chapter. This analysis is particularly important if you are losing money now or think sales may decline in the future. The only way to maximize profits and avoid losing money is to reduce fixed costs.

Chapter 15 describes how to determine the advisability of acquiring additional fixed assets. Most equipment purchases involve a large amount of money and a fairly long-term repayment commitment. Mistakes are potentially expensive to correct, so at least a minimum amount of analysis is helpful to avoid ill-advised acquisitions.

Chapter 16 describes how to finance your business. Since banks are the most common source of financing for small businesses, this chapter discusses how to deal with your banker and lists the key rules you should follow to ensure a harmonious relationship.

Chapter 17 wraps all of this together into a description of how to complete and implement a comprehensive business and financial plan for your business.

This book takes mysterious, complex financial theories out of the classroom and into the day-to-day setting of your business. Implementing these concepts is the key to achieving financial success, and successful implementation of the financial management concepts outlined in this book will place you in the top one or two percent of all business owners who struggle with this on a continuing basis.

According to the National Federation of Independent Business, 80 percent of business owners are not satisfied with either their return on investment or the degree of financial success they have achieved. This book is about changing those results. Study it well, and you will learn how to define, measure, and achieve financial success in your business!

David A. Duryee, Managing Principal
Management Advisory Services
A Division of Moss Adams

Acknowledgments

No effort of this kind is the work of just one person. I would espe-cially like to thank Bob Hogan, senior manager of Management Advisory Services, for his untiring efforts to help with layout and conceptual issues. I think it is safe to say that this book would not have been published without his help.

Mark Tibergien and Steve Cranfill, co-principals of Manage-ment Advisory Services, were also very helpful in the develop-ment of this book, and I am very grateful for their editorial comments, which added greatly to the ultimate readability.

I would be remiss if I did not thank my wife Anne, for enduring many husbandless nights and weekends without a word of complaint.

Finally, I would like to thank the thousands of business owners whom I have had the pleasure of meeting over the years. It takes a lot of courage and mental toughness to plow ahead in your own business against stiff odds, and they never cease to be a source of tremendous inspiration.

Contents

Chapter One

Introduction

F inancial success. It has a nice ring to it. It is what those of us who own a business are striving to attain. There are, of course, all kinds of philosophical reasons for being in business— for example, wanting to help others and providing a superior product or service. But you are taking a fairly sizable risk by starting your own business, and you should ultimately be adequately compensated for taking this risk. This book is all about how to define, measure, and achieve financial success in your business.

The statistics are not encouraging. Over 85 percent of all businesses fail within the first ten years of their existence. What causes this alarmingly high failure rate? The overwhelming majority fail due to *bad management*, and frequently this translates into bad *financial* management.

Experience tells us that the most common reasons for failure are:

1. *Lack of financial planning.* Business owners tend not to be great planners. They are action-oriented people who do not focus much attention on the next few years.

2. *Absence of timely and accurate business records.* Hiring professionals to provide financial statements is expensive. Who needs all that paper? Many owners reason that a shoebox full of receipts should be sufficient.

3. *Lack of understanding of financial statements.* Even if the financial statements are prepared, they are often confusing and difficult to understand (more evidence that they are not really needed).

4. *Poor cash flow management.* So what needs to be managed? Cash comes in one pocket and goes out the other. That's pretty simple and straightforward.

5. *Poor debt management.* How much is enough? Too much? Where should it come from? How should it be structured? How and when can it be paid back?
6. *Lack of knowledge of costs.* Most business owners have no idea what it costs to deliver their products or services. Pricing is therefore unsophisticated and may not allow sufficient profit margins.

Most people who start businesses do so because they know how to do something, make something, or sell something. They probably do not have a very strong background in finance, and conversations with accountants, bankers, or financial consultants can sometimes be confusing. Without intending to, these people often speak their own language and use unfamiliar terms that intimidate us.

So business owners tend to take a fairly simplistic approach to financial management. As long as the business is growing and profitable, everything is OK. If a lot of sales and profits are good, then more is even better. If things are not going well today, then tomorrow they will surely improve.

Effective financial management of a business is much more involved than that, but *it does not need to be complicated.* On a step-by-step basis, anyone, no matter what his or her prior background, can learn how to do it.

FINANCIAL PHASES OF YOUR BUSINESS

While the general principles of effective financial management remain constant, the financial environment of your business will probably change over time. Businesses typically experience four distinct phases as they grow: start-up, high growth, mature, and decline/renewal. Each phase has somewhat different financial needs and characteristics, so it will be helpful to identify which phase your business is in as you apply this book to your business.

Growth in sales starts out slowly, accelerates rapidly, then slows down, and eventually flattens out, according to the following diagram.

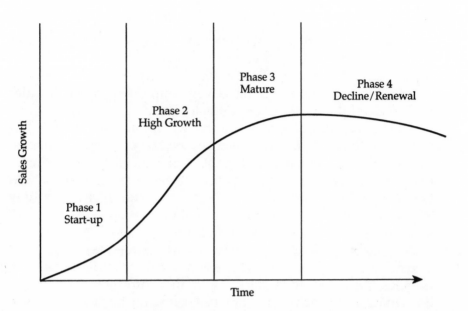

Phase 1: Start-Up

Entrepreneurs who start businesses have a vision and are driven to making it a reality. They do not, however, usually have much money. This initial phase of business, the start-up phase, is typically characterized by the following:

1. A lack of capital.
2. Poor or nonexistent cash flow.
3. Management that lacks experience in running a business.
4. Poor financial information.

These deficiencies account for the fact that no one really wants to have much to do with business owners in this phase. They are usually the outcasts of the business world. Bankers run the other way fast and relatives even faster. Venture capitalists don't even look at 80 percent of the deals submitted to them and turn down more than half of the rest. Established businesses hesitate to offer credit for fear that they will not collect what is due.

Start-up is a difficult phase. Survival is constantly in question, and the work is neverending. This is sometimes called the wonder phase of business, because most of the time you wonder if you are going to make it and the rest of the time you wonder why you ever started in the first place. If you had known how hard it was going to be, you probably would never have attempted it.

Effective financial planning is very important in the wonder phase. Careful financial projections for the first few years of business can determine how much capital will ultimately be needed. If it is more than can be scrounged by whatever means available, then it would be wise to postpone starting. A realistic projection of future cash flow is essential if you will need to borrow money. At best it will be difficult to do; without projections, it is probably impossible. Implementing the information contained in chapters 7 through 10 is very important in the wonder phase.

Profitability is also a problem for a start-up business. It is critical to reach at least a break-even position. Chapter 11 describes how to calculate break-even sales. With this information, you can determine how much you might lose before the business begins to generate a profit.

Phase 2: High Growth

Sheer hard work, guts, and determination are often enough to get you through the wonder phase, and in phase II things begin to get exciting. Sales and profits take off. This phase is typically characterized by the following:

1. High growth in sales and profits.
2. Highly strained capital.
3. Negative cash flow.
4. Transition management.
5. Marginal financial records.

Starting from a fairly low level, sales and profits grow at a rapid rate. Cash flow, however, is terrible. It seems as if the more you advance, the more you fall behind. Capital is strained to the breaking point, and borrowing sources are quickly overextended.

Management is gaining experience in running the business. But it may not be able to make the transition successfully from seat of the pants management to the more professional, structured approach required for a rapidly growing business.

Things in general begin to get out of hand. Mistakes are made. Wrong things are done at the wrong time. This is sometimes called the blunder phase, and the business may or may not survive the cumulative impact of all of the mistakes that are made.

This is the phase where many businesses fail. They literally grow themselves broke and collapse due to poor cash flow and excessive debt, just when things start to look promising.

Cash flow is usually a significant problem, and it needs to be monitored very carefully. Projections for income statements, balance sheets, and cash flow are essential. You cannot expect the bank, or any other source of credit, to provide all that you might need in this phase.

That's the bad news. The good news is that you can avoid the worst blunders by applying the financial management techniques described in this book. While success is not guaranteed, they will help you to navigate through the blunder phase and join the 15 percent of businesses that make it to the next phase.

Phase 3: Mature

This is the phase that you dream about. You have finally arrived. There is more cash coming in than going out, and you can begin to enjoy the fruits of your sacrifice and hard work. It is time to join the right clubs, vacation at the right places, trade in the compact car for a luxury model, and pay yourself a big salary. Financial success has been achieved.

Typical characteristics of this phase follow:

1. Strong capital.
2. Positive cash flow.
3. Experienced management.
4. Timely and accurate financial information.

Since you have survived the wars and joined the small minority of people who make it to this phase, you feel pretty smart. You have developed answers for most of the problems facing the world and are more than happy to share them with others—even without being asked. You have a whole new attitude when you go to the bank. Your hat is squarely on your head, not in your hand,

and you expect the red carpet treatment. This is sometimes called the thunder phase. Well, you're entitled to thunder. You're successful, and you want others to know it.

Information is probably very good now. Both capital and cash flow are strong. Top management is experienced and there are second-line specialists in such areas as sales, marketing, production, and finance.

Now that you've arrived in the thunder phase, your goal is to stay there, but this may not be easy. Growth is only moderate at this point, and you need to be careful that competing firms do not grow at a faster rate and shrink your share of the market. Complacency and/or overconfidence may be a problem. As management ages, it may become too conservative. Maturity is a great phase to be in, but it takes careful planning to stay there.

A word of caution. Toward the end of the blunder phase, the business is very profitable but still does not have good cash flow. Entering the thunder phase prematurely and spending money you really don't have usually has disastrous consequences. Be cautious about how and when you thunder, and make sure that your actions do not have a crippling impact on your business. Careful monitoring of your financial condition is especially important in the thunder phase.

Phase 4: Decline/Renewal

Like the wonder phase, decline/renewal is a hard time in the life of a business. Managers are now in their late 50s or early 60s, and age has become a partner in the business.

The desire to take risks is gone. Conservation of existing assets is the primary theme, and younger employees or family members chafe at the lack of growth or direction. This phase is characterized by the following:

1. Adequate capital.
2. Positive cash flow.
3. Indifferent management.
4. Underutilized financial information.

Market share begins to decline as more aggressive firms grow faster than yours. Cash flow and profitability are still adequate but declining. The company begins to feed on itself and use up its accumulated resources. This is sometimes called the plunder phase[1] of business.

It is probably time for the older group to step aside and let the business launch into another high-growth phase. This is often difficult, however, both emotionally and financially.

A business in the plunder phase can either go down and eventually out or renew and achieve high growth, repeating the blunder phase. This new blunder phase will not be nearly as difficult or uncertain as the first one, but it is important for the ultimate survival of the business. A careful analysis of the available resources, long-term financial planning, and good succession planning are essential in the plunder phase.

SUMMARY

Think about your phase of business as you read through this book. Actions, attitudes, and challenges in the development of your business differ for each phase, but one thing is certain: the financial principles and techniques in the ensuing chapters will always help you achieve financial success.

Good luck in your thunder quest!

---

[1] Dr. Leon Danco coined the colorful terms wonder, blunder, thunder, and plunder for the four phases of business in his book *Beyond Survival*.

Chapter Two

Overview

E ffective financial management can be very intimidating. It is a
lot of work and involves concepts that are only vaguely familiar to most business owners. The key to simplifying this effort is to
take one step at a time. Do not be discouraged by looking at the
entire task, and do not proceed with the next step until you have
completed the current one.

There are four distinct steps in the financial management
process:

1. Historical analysis.
2. Long-range plan.
3. Short-range plan.
4. Implementation.

HISTORICAL ANALYSIS

The following steps are involved in the historical analysis process:

1. Spread your financial statements.
2. Calculate the common size percentages.
3. Calculate the key financial relationships (ratios).
4. Analyze cash flow.
5. Examine trends and compare to industry averages.
6. Identify problems or areas of concern.
7. List solutions.

Step 1: Spread Your Financial Statements

First, put the data from four or five years of balance sheets on one page. (Do the same for income statements). Spreading your financial statements allows you to look at accounts side by side over several years and spot trends that you might not otherwise notice. It also makes the information much easier to work with as you analyze the history of your business.

Step 2: Calculate Common Size Percentages

For the balance sheets, each asset, liability, and equity account is divided by total assets. This is called a *common size analysis* because you will then be able to compare your balance sheets to others in your industry on a percentage basis. For the income statements, divide all expense accounts by total sales. This allows you to determine if expenses are growing faster than sales (which is almost always undesirable).

Step 3: Calculate Key Ratios

The next step is to calculate some key relationships that are called *ratios*. The idea is to look not just at the numbers themselves but at what they are in *relation* to something else. In this way you can measure specific areas of your business such as liquidity, safety, profitability, operating performance, and cash flow.

Step 4: Analyze Cash Flow

If your financial statements are prepared according to generally accepted accounting principles (GAAP), your accountant will either provide you with a statement of cash flow or add a disclaimer that such a document was not prepared.

In the statement, cash flow is separated into three distinct areas: operating cash flow, investing cash flow, and financing cash flow. You should be knowledgeable about these three types of cash flow and how they are behaving in your business.

Step 5: Examine Trends and Industry Averages

Once you have calculated ratios to analyze liquidity, safety, profitability, operating performance, and cash flow, trends should be analyzed and comparisons made to industry averages.

Step 6: Identify Problems

You will be surprised and pleased to find out that you do not need an MBA to spot problems. After steps 1 through 5, they will be obvious.

Step 7: Determine Solutions

More good news! The solutions will be obvious also. That does not mean, however, that they will be easy.

LONG-RANGE PLAN

A long-range financial plan is typically for three years, but this can vary depending on the type of business. An aircraft manufacturer, for example, must plan at least ten years ahead, but a small clothing retailer may be able to see only one to two years into the future.

For most businesses three years is appropriate, so a three-year planning period will be used for illustrative purposes throughout this book.

To establish your long-range financial plan:

1. Project income statements.
2. Project balance sheets.
3. Project cash flow.
4. Project ratios.

The income statements are projected first. Once this has been accomplished, the balance sheets can be projected. Following that, you can calculate the cash flow and ratios.

The long-range financial plan gives you a road map to follow in determining whether you are following the right path toward financial success. Each year, update the plan and extend it out another year. You will always have a long-range financial plan in place, guiding you toward your financial goals.

SHORT-RANGE PLAN

The third step in the financial management process is to project the first year of your long-range plan on a monthly basis.

1. Determine your monthly sales pattern.
2. Project monthly expenses.
3. Determine cash flow assumptions.
4. Project monthly cash flow.

The short-range plan allows you to monitor the progress toward your goal each month and take appropriate corrective action when necessary. It would obviously be too late if you waited until the end of the year to find out that your annual goals had not been achieved.

More importantly, if your business has any seasonality at all (that is, if sales are not spread evenly throughout the year), you must plan carefully for the impact this will have on your monthly cash flow.

If cash outflow is greater than cash inflow, you must plan for how or where this will be made up in your business. You must also estimate how large the cumulative deficit cash flow will be, when it will peak, and when (or if) you will be able to pay it all back.

Having this plan in hand will greatly enhance your communications with your bank. You will be able to describe how your business will operate in the coming year and the role you need the bank to play. Of course, your underlying assumptions may be questioned, but your banker will respond enthusiastically to this type of information.

Two other aspects of effective financial management are important, managing for profits and analyzing fixed asset acquisitions.

Managing for Profits

Managing for profits involves determining your fixed and variable costs. It is an analysis of how costs behave in your business. It is important to pay constant attention to fixed costs, because it is amazingly easy for them to inch upward and erode your profitability.

If your sales are declining, you should be strategizing well in advance about which fixed costs should be cut and when. This will maximize profitability and avoid or at least minimize future losses.

Fixed Asset Acquisitions

Analyzing fixed asset acquisitions is an exercise that is not well understood or implemented in most businesses, but it is important in order to avoid potentially costly mistakes.

Determining when or if to purchase fixed assets is a financial decision. Emotions and gut instinct will probably not serve you well. Each investment in fixed assets should earn an appropriate return. Make each of your purchases pass the financial test outlined in this book, and you will be well on your way to maximizing the return on investment in your business.

IMPLEMENTING THE PLAN

The final and most important step in the financial management process is implementing the financial plan.

There may be a great temptation to put this plan on a shelf once it is completed. Creating it was a fair amount of work and took a lot of time. You are pleased that it is done and you don't want to see it again for a while. But if you put it aside, all your effort was wasted.

There are no awards for prize-winning plans that sit on the shelf gathering dust. You will not be nominated for any business planning hall of fame. The only reward comes from making sure you have done your best to make the plan really happen. This requires constant monitoring and effort.

Each month, determine what actually happened, what you thought was doing to happen, and the difference (called a positive or negative *variance*). Then take corrective action. This will ensure that your financial plan is not just a paper effort but actually assists you in the day-to-day operation of your business.

SUMMARY

Running a financially successful business is hard work. There are no shortcuts. There are also no excuses. Decide today that you will be among the 15 percent who survive.

Read this book, and then make financial success happen in your business!

Chapter Three

Balance Sheet Analysis

E ffective financial management is important regardless of your phase of business. But where do you begin? How do you make any sense out of the jumble of numbers and mysterious jargon that accountants and other number crunchers throw at you? This stuff is not your game.

This chapter begins the process of describing how to analyze the historical financial results of your business. Financial terms with which you should be familiar will be defined in nontechnical language. Reasons for performing each step will be given. The text will assume that you know little about business finance.

CONTENTS OF THE BALANCE SHEET

The balance sheet is always the first financial statement you get from your certified public accountant (CPA), so that is where our analysis begins. The balance sheet is a statement of assets, liabilities, and equity. *Equity* is the accounting term for the funds that are claimed by the owner of the business after all of the funds owed to creditors are subtracted from total assets. Net worth, net book value, and net investment all mean the same thing, but equity will be used throughout this book. The balance sheet is referred to as a position statement because it shows the amount of assets, liabilities, and equity on a particular date.

Assets are what you own, such as accounts receivable, inventory, and equipment. *Liabilities* are what you owe, such as accounts payable, bank loans, and mortgages. Equity is whatever is left after you subtract the liabilities from the assets:

Assets	−	Liabilities	=	Equity
what you own		what you owe		what's left for you

Stated another way, the basic formula for the balance sheet is

| Assets | = | Liabilities | + | Equity |

Total funds invested = Funds supplied by + Funds supplied by
    in the business   creditors   owners

The following diagram illustrates a typical balance sheet. Notice that the assets are separated into current and fixed assets and the liabilities are separated into current and long-term liabilities.

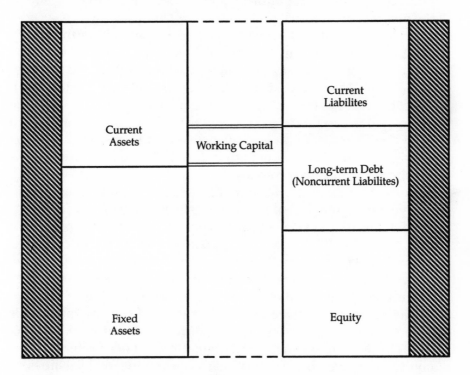

Current assets are those assets that are likely to turn to cash within one year from the date of the balance sheet. They are listed in order of their liquidity (or nearness to cash). Examples include cash, accounts receivable, inventory, and prepaid expenses. (*Prepaid expenses* may seem like a contradiction in terms. How can something be an asset and an expense at the same time? This account refers to cash that is paid *in advance* for things like rent, interest, and insurance. The payment is initially set up as an asset and then written off as an expense over the appropriate period.)

Fixed assets include such items as land, building, furniture, fixtures, equipment, and leasehold improvements. Note that fixed assets are usually listed on your balance sheet at cost. Actually, the rule is cost or market, whichever is lower. Therefore, if the current market value of your land were to drop below its cost, your CPA would reduce its value on your balance sheet. This is not often done, due to the difficulty in determining market value in the absence of an actual sale.

Valuing your assets for balance sheet presentation can be very complex, especially in the area of inventory. Inventory can be accounted for on the basis of last in, first out (LIFO), first in, first out (FIFO), average cost, or other methods. Each method will affect the value of the inventory on your balance sheet. If you have any questions about the values on your balance sheet, continue to ask your CPA until you are satisfied with the answers. (Getting the maximum benefit from your accountant often requires knowing the right questions to ask.)

Current liabilities are those that are due or must be paid within one year from the date of the balance sheet. They include accounts payable, notes payable, accrued expenses, and current portion of long-term debt. They are normally listed in declining order of their maturity (with the ones due soonest listed first).

Long-term liabilities are those that are due after 12 months. They include mortgages and other long-term notes payable.

The difference between current assets and current liabilities is called *working capital* (sometimes referred to as net working capital). This is distinguished from regular capital (also referred to as equity or net worth), which is total assets minus total liabilities.

Note how the assets on the left side of the diagram are financed with the liabilities and equity on the right side. Part of the current assets are financed with current liabilities, and part of them (the working capital part) are financed with long-term liabilities or equity. All of the fixed assets are financed with either long-term liabilities or equity.

Examine this diagram carefully. Make sure that you do not make the mistake of financing long-term needs (working capital and fixed assets) on a short-term basis (with current liabilities).

Such misfinancing will reduce your company's liquidity (which is defined in the next section).

What does the balance sheet tell you? What do you want to learn from it? Many business owners make the mistake of looking at the numbers on the balance sheet and trying to arrive at meaningful conclusions. How much do you have in total assets? How much is your equity? Has it gone up from the prior period?

These questions sound important, but they are really not. In fact, looking at the numbers may lead you to erroneous conclusions about the financial condition of your business. What is important is how much your equity is in *relation* to something else. Or how much your assets are in *relation* to something else. These relationships, or *ratios*, are very helpful in determining the historical financial condition of your business. They are routinely used by bankers and other analysts for that purpose.

Obviously, there are other factors you should consider—for example, the quality of management and the company's competitive position in the marketplace. However, this book focuses on the relevant ratios, what they measure, and how you should apply them to your business. When you determine where you have been and where you need to go based on the financial standards you have established for these ratios, you will be well on your way to achieving financial success in your business.

You want to learn two things from the balance sheet through examining the appropriate ratios: liquidity and safety.

Liquidity

Liquidity is defined here as the ability to pay bills. It is a way to quantify whether your business can satisfactorily pay its short-term obligations. This analysis will allow you to determine if you are becoming more or less liquid, or if you are meeting the standards of liquidity that you have established for your business.

Since current assets are those assets that will turn to cash within one year, and current liabilities are those obligations that are due within one year, it makes sense that if you compare one to the other, you will get an indication of your company's ability to pay its short-term obligations.

Liquidity is calculated as follows:

Current assets
—————————————
Current liabilities

This is called the current ratio. It is a test of liquidity, the ability to pay bills. In interpreting this ratio, it is helpful to put a dollar sign on it. If, for example, you have a current ratio of 1.53 to 1 (the "1" is always left off in expressing these ratios), you would have $1.53 of current assets to pay every $1.00 of current liabilities. Most industry averages for the current ratio range between 1.50 and 1.90. Industry averages and management standards for these ratios will be discussed later in this book.

A more stringent test for liquidity is to compare just the cash and accounts receivable to current liabilities. This comparison relates those assets that are likely to turn to cash within the next 90 days to the current liabilities (most of which are probably due within 90 days).

It is calculated as follows:

Cash + Accounts receivable
———————————————————————————
Current liabilities

This is called the quick ratio, since the assets are more quickly convertible to cash. (If you have marketable securities on your balance sheet that are truly marketable, they can be added to the cash and accounts receivable in calculating this ratio.)

Again, it is helpful to put a dollar sign on this ratio. If you have a quick ratio of 0.84 to 1, you would have $0.84 in quick assets (cash, accounts receivable, and marketable securities) to pay every $1.00 in current liabilities. Most industry averages for the quick ratio will range between 0.70 and 0.90. It's not a problem that they are less than one, because not all current liabilities are due within 90 days.

The current ratio and the quick ratio measure the liquidity of your business.

It should be noted here that service businesses typically do not have inventory (which is the primary asset excluded from the quick ratio), so their quick ratio tends to be very similar to their current ratio. For this reason, calculating the quick ratio for service companies is not that informative. It is therefore common to rely on the current ratio to measure liquidity for service businesses.

Safety

Safety is defined here as the ability to withstand adversity. Adversity may be anything from a downturn in the economy to a natural disaster of some sort.

You can measure safety by comparing total liabilities (debt) to equity, because the firms that have the heaviest debt load in relation to their equity at the time of the adversity are the least likely to survive.

The ratio measuring safety is therefore:

Total liabilities
_____
  Equity

This is called the *debt to equity ratio.* It is a basic financial principle that the more you rely on debt versus equity to finance your business, the more risk you face. Therefore the higher the debt to equity ratio, the less safe is your business.

If you apply a dollar sign to this ratio, a debt to equity ratio of 2.25 would mean that there is $2.25 in liabilities for every $1.00 of equity, or that the creditors have a little over twice as much invested in the business as does the owner. Most industry averages range from 1.50 to 2.00. Some industries, such as real estate, restaurants, and automobile dealers, tend to have much higher averages.

The debt to equity ratio is one of the most important ratios examined by your banker, who is always concerned about the riskiness of your business. If this ratio gets too high, then you will become a much less desirable loan prospect. (Anything 3.00 or higher is usually a red flag for your banker.) A high debt to equity ratio indicates that additional equity is needed in order to keep risk within reasonable limits.

How do you determine the "right" amount of risk for your business? This depends on several factors:

1. *Your individual tolerance for risk.* This will be different for every person and will probably change as your situation changes (age, family, etc.).
2. *The type of business.* Some activities, such as investment in real estate, may be able to tolerate a higher amount of debt than others. It is not common to pay cash for a building, for example.

3. *The status of the economy.* If a downturn or recession is expected, it would be wise to pay off debt and make your balance sheet less vulnerable during the tough times. Conversely, if a strong economy is expected, then it may be a good time to aggressively expand your business and take on more debt in the process. Risk will be higher, but that is all right when no adversity is anticipated.

4. *The status of the industry.* If your industry is in a downturn, this may not be a good time to increase debt. On the other hand, if your debt to equity ratio is very low at the time of a downturn, it can be an advantageous time to expand aggressively, acquire other firms (perhaps at a depressed price), and take on additional debt.

5. *The age of the business owner.* As a general rule, older business owners are less interested in taking risk (the term *older* is used advisedly in this instance and is deliberately not defined). They want to make sure their money survives as long as they do. This is not a time for taking big risks.

A thorough understanding of the principle of safety and risk is important for every business owner. This does not mean that risk is always bad and safety always good. There are times when risk is appropriate—or, indeed, unavoidable. The point is that you should choose carefully when to go heavily into debt and monitor the safety of your business on a regular basis. This will ensure that you are operating within your tolerance for accepting risk and in a fashion consistent with your goals of survival.

BALANCE SHEET ADJUSTMENTS

Your assets are listed on your balance sheet at cost, less depreciation, if any. They may therefore be considerably understated compared to their actual market value. If you feel this is the case with your business, adjust the value of your assets upward and then recalculate these ratios.

This should be done with care and caution, since actual market values are difficult to determine with precision. In any case, always calculate the ratios from the values stated on your balance sheet first so that you will have ratios that are comparable to industry averages.

TREND ANALYSIS

Examining your balance sheet for just one period may be misleading. To avoid this, look at the trends over a period of years. Your business may have low liquidity currently but be improving each year. Or it may have good but deteriorating safety. A trend analysis is therefore an important part of the analysis process.

INDUSTRY COMPARISONS

Whenever possible, it is desirable to look at ratio comparisons for similar businesses. The point is not necessarily to emulate everyone else, but it is valuable to see where you are in relation to others in your industry and where you differ from them. Are you different in a good or bad way? Are you different on purpose or accidentally? Are you different because of the unique aspects of your business and its location? These questions are important to answer as you look at industry averages.

Where do you find industry comparisons? One primary publication that contains data for many industries is *Annual Statement Studies*, published annually by Robert Morris Associates (RMA). Your banker or your library will have a copy of this publication; make a point to see if your industry is included. If not, then other sources may be helpful, such as Dun & Bradstreet or a ratio study done by your trade association. (If such a study does not exist, write to your association president and suggest that one be done.) Ask your librarian for help on this. Any information you discover will be helpful in effectively analyzing your ratios.

MANAGEMENT STANDARDS

Once you have become familiar with these ratios in your business and what they mean, you will want to set your own standards. You can decide how risky you want your business to be and then manage your debt accordingly. If you want to routinely take advantage of trade discounts by paying your bills within ten days, then you are going to require fairly high current and quick ratios. Industry averages are interesting, but your own standards are much more meaningful for your business.

CASH VERSUS ACCRUAL ACCOUNTING

As you go through this book, you need to be aware that there are two different accounting systems that you can operate under: the cash or accrual system. The information and case studies contained in this book are all based on accrual accounting information. But not all businesses follow this procedure.

The recognition of revenue and expenses is the main distinction between the cash and accrual systems. Under cash basis accounting, revenue is not recognized until cash is received, and expenses are not recognized until cash is paid. In accrual accounting, revenue is recognized at the time of sale, whether cash is received or not, and expenses are recognized when incurred, whether cash is paid or not. Farms, fishing ventures, service firms, and restaurants are examples of businesses that are typically on a cash basis of accounting.

The primary impact of cash basis accounting is that your balance sheet will not contain any accounts receivable or accounts payable, despite the fact that you may have both. The result is that your balance sheet may be grossly distorted. To avoid this distortion, all businesses that are on cash basis accounting should routinely ask their accountant or bookkeeper to prepare accrual basis financial statements. You can pay taxes based on cash basis accounting, but you must manage your business based on accrual accounting. It's that simple.

CASE STUDY: DURGAN ELECTRIC CO.

The rest of this book will describe and explain financial management principles utilizing a case study of Durgan Electric Co., a wholesaler of industrial and consumer electrical supplies. Sales are to contractors and retail hardware stores. Bob Durgan, 67, is the owner of the business; his son Mark, 41, is the sales manager. The company was founded by Bob and has been in business for many years.

Don't be concerned if you are in a different industry. The principles discussed in this text are generic in nature and apply to you as well as to Durgan. There are certain peculiarities in analyzing a service business, and these will be pointed out where appropriate. Obviously, if you have no inventory, then you can skip the part about analyzing inventory. Everything else will apply to you.

The next page illustrates the balance sheets for Durgan Electric for the past three years. Three years of historical financial statements will be used throughout this book for ease of discussing various principles. However, the reader is urged to use at least five years in performing this analysis.

Spreading the balance sheets like this on one piece of paper is the first step in the analysis process. Industry averages for Durgan refer to the numbers published by RMA for wholesalers of electrical supplies.

Common Size Analysis

Another analysis of your balance sheet in addition to the ratios listed earlier allows comparison to prior periods or to others in your industry on a common basis. A *common size analysis* involves dividing all of your asset, liability, and equity accounts by total assets. This shows what each asset, liability, and equity account is as a percentage of total assets.

This analysis is a good exercise for you to do at least annually, whether you compare your business to others or not. You can easily see, for example, if your inventory or accounts receivable are becoming a larger percentage of total assets. This is probably not desirable.

Your accountant may routinely provide these calculations on your annual balance sheet. He or she will certainly do so if requested.

The percentage columns on the Durgan balance sheets reflect the common size calculations. You can make the following observations from those calculations:

1. Cash has doubled as a percentage of total assets, from 10.9 percent to 20.1 percent.
2. Accounts receivable has declined from 36.4 percent to 27.2 percent.

Durgan Electric Co.
Balance Sheet Spread
($000s)

	19X1		19X2		19X3	
Assets						
Cash	$ 194	10.9%	$ 320	18.3%	$ 347	20.1%
Accounts receivable	650	36.4	570	32.5	470	27.2
Inventory	676	37.8	580	33.1	636	36.8
Prepaid expenses	8	0.4	9	0.5	11	0.6
Total current assets	$1,528	85.5	$1,479	84.4	$1,464	84.7
Leasehold improvements	93	5.2	93	5.3	93	5.4
Furniture and equipment	769	43.0	831	47.5	876	50.7
Gross fixed assets	862	48.2	924	52.8	969	56.1
Less: Depreciation	(602)	(33.7)	(652)	(37.2)	(705)	(40.8)
Net fixed assets	260	14.5	272	15.6	264	15.3
Total Assets	**$1,788**	**100.0**	**$1,751**	**100.0**	**$1,728**	**100.0**
Liabilities						
Notes payable, bank	$ 0	0.0	$ 0	0.0	$ 0	0.0
Accounts payable, trade	451	25.2	359	20.5	381	22.0
Accrued expenses	38	2.1	21	1.2	20	1.2
Total current liabilities	$ 489	27.3	$ 380	21.7	$ 401	23.2
Long-term debt	186	10.4	208	11.9	123	7.1
Total Liabilities	**$ 675**	**37.7**	**$ 588**	**33.6**	**$ 524**	**30.3**
Equity						
Stock	75	4.2	75	4.3	75	4.3
Retained earnings	1,038	58.1	1,088	62.1	1,129	65.4
Total Equity	**$1,113**	**62.3**	**$1,163**	**66.4**	**$1,204**	**69.7**
Total Liabilities and Equity	**$1,788**	**100.0**	**$1,751**	**100.0**	**$1,728**	**100.0**

3. Equity has increased from 62.3 percent to 69.7 percent.

4. All other accounts have remained relatively constant over the three-year period as percentages of total assets.

There is nothing particularly alarming about these observations, although you might conclude that the business is carrying excess cash at the present time. While this may be a nice problem to have, cash does not generate much in the way of income and needs to be managed accordingly. Too much cash or liquidity will have a depressing impact on earnings in most cases.

Liquidity

The following are the current and quick ratios for Durgan for the periods 19X1 through 19X3:

	19X1	19X2	19X3	Industry Average
Current ratio	3.12	3.89	3.65	1.95
Quick ratio	1.73	2.34	2.04	0.90

The current ratio for 19X3 of 3.65 means that the company has $3.65 of current assets to pay every $1.00 of current liabilities. The trend is up since 19X1. Durgan's current ratio is much higher than the industry comparison of 1.95 ($1.95 of current assets to pay every $1.00 of current liabilities).

The quick ratio for 19X3 of 2.04 means that the company has $2.04 of quick assets (cash and accounts receivable) to pay every $1.00 of current liabilities. The trend is up since 19X1. Durgan's quick ratio is quite a bit higher than the industry comparison of 0.90 ($0.90 of quick assets to pay every $1.00 of current liabilities).

From this analysis, you can conclude that the liquidity of this company is excellent in 19X3 and has improved since 19X1.

Safety

The following are the debt to equity ratios for Durgan for the periods 19X1 through 19X3:

	19X1	19X2	19X3	Industry Average
Debt to equity ratio	0.61	0.51	0.44	1.30

The ratio of 0.44 in 19X3 means that the company has $0.44 in debt for every dollar of equity. This has been trending downward since 19X1 and is quite a bit less than the industry comparison of 1.30 ($1.30 of debt for every dollar of equity).

The conclusion is that this company is very safe in 19X3 and is getting safer, as evidenced by the declining debt to equity ratio.

Financial Impact Analysis

Another important use of the ratios is determining the dollar financial impact of your performance, as reflected by the ratios you have calculated. For example, a question for Durgan might be how much can debt increase without incurring more risk than the industry as a whole? This process is called *financial impact analysis*. The total liability impact can be calculated as follows:

$$\text{Equity} \times \frac{\text{Target debt to}}{\text{equity ratio}} = \text{Target liabilities}$$

$$\$1,204,000 \times 1.30 \qquad = \$1,565,000$$

$$\text{Target liabilities} - \text{Actual liabilities} = \text{Financial impact}$$

$$\$1,565,000 - \$524,000 \qquad = \$1,041,400$$

This means that Durgan Electric can increase debt by $1,041,000 without the debt to equity ratio increasing beyond the industry average of 1.30.

Refer to Table 7–1 for a complete list of financial impact analysis formulas.

This concludes our analysis of Durgan's balance sheets. It began with a spread of several years' statements and included a common size analysis and a measurement of liquidity (ability to pay bills) and safety (ability to withstand adversity). Three ratios (current, quick, and debt to equity) were used to measure liquidity and safety.

Our conclusion is that the balance sheets for Durgan are very strong. The company is both liquid and safe. The trends are good, and the company compares very favorably to industry averages (as published by Robert Morris Associates in *Annual Statement Studies*). There is nothing to indicate any cause for alarm at this point.

SUMMARY

There are two things that you want the balance sheet to tell you: liquidity, the ability to pay bills; and safety, the ability to withstand adversity. Liquidity is measured by the current and quick ratios, and safety is measured by the debt to equity ratio.

Trends are very important in analyzing these ratios, as are industry averages and the financial impact analysis. A common size analysis is also helpful in determining the trend of your assets, liabilities, and equity as a percentage of total assets. This analysis will allow you to compare your balance sheets on a common size basis with others in your industry.

Remember that the ratios should also be calculated using values for assets that have been adjusted to fair market value versus book value, if appropriate. This may give different results, particularly for the debt to equity ratio.

The next chapter will describe how to analyze the income statement and measure profitability.

Chapter Four

Income Statement Analysis

W e have determined that the balance sheets reflect both the liquidity and safety of the business. We measure these not by looking at the numbers themselves but by looking at some key relationships. By looking at just three ratios (the current, quick, and debt to equity ratios), we are able to determine liquidity (ability to pay bills) and safety (ability to withstand adversity). Both trends and comparisons to industry averages are also important.

CONTENTS OF THE INCOME STATEMENT

The next step in the historical analysis process is to measure profitability by analyzing income statements. The *income statement* is a statement of sales, expenses, and profit. It is referred to as a period statement since it covers a particular period of time (usually month, quarter, or year). The diagram on the next page illustrates the format of a typical income statement.

Expenses are separated into cost of goods sold and operating expenses. Operating expenses are also referred to as overhead or general and administrative expenses.

Cost of goods sold usually consists of such things as direct labor, raw materials, freight, and factory operating expenses. These are expenses that are *directly* related to the production of the sales. They are distinguished from such expenses as legal, accounting, travel, entertainment, insurance, and advertising, which are part of operating expenses. Depreciation on factory equipment is often included in cost of goods sold.

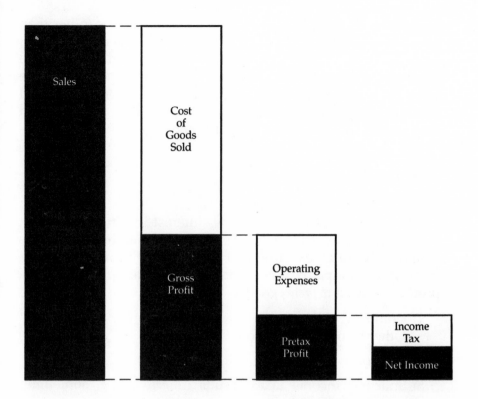

Whether you include commissions or other selling expenses in cost of goods sold is a matter of personal preference. These expenses are sometimes separately identified under operating expense as selling expense, in order to track them more closely.

Sales minus cost of goods sold equals *gross profit*. This is the same as gross margin, but gross profit will be used throughout this book.

Sales
 − Cost of goods sold
Gross profit

Note in the diagram that gross profit is all that is available to pay operating expenses and generate an operating profit. Gross profit is therefore very important in determining the overall profitability of your business.

Operating expenses consist of such items as salaries (other than direct labor), advertising, rent, travel, entertainment, insurance, legal services, office supplies, accounting, bad debts, auto expenses, dues, and subscriptions. Operating expenses are the same as overhead expenses, indirect expenses, or general and administrative expenses. When operating expenses are subtracted from gross profit, the result is *operating profit*.

Gross profit
− Operating expenses

Operating profit

Other income and expense includes interest income or expense, gain or loss on the sale of an asset, and other nonrecurring gains or losses. These are expenses that are *not* part of the normal operations of the company. When they are subtracted from operating profit, the result is *pretax profit*.

Operating profit
− Other income and expense

Pretax profit

Subtracting income taxes results in *net income*, sometimes referred to as net profit after tax or after-tax profit.

Pretax profit
− Income tax

Net income

The full outline of the income statement is therefore:

Sales
− Cost of goods sold

Gross profit
− Operating expense

Operating profit
+ / − Other income/expense

Pretax profit
− Income tax

Net income

To measure profitability, we need to look at key relationships rather than the numbers. What you have in sales or profits in *relationship to something else* is what is important.

Two ratios (stated as percentages) are used to measure profitability. They are the gross profit ratio and the pretax profit ratio.

The gross profit ratio is

$$\frac{\text{Gross profit}}{\text{Sales}}$$

The gross profit ratio is one of the most important ratios that you will calculate. This is the front line of attack in your business. If you lose the battle here, then you have no real opportunity to make it up elsewhere in your income statement. Your gross profit is therefore critical. A deviation of even a fraction of one percent can be very detrimental to your operating profit.

The pretax profit ratio is

$$\frac{\text{Pretax profit}}{\text{Sales}}$$

The pretax profit ratio is important to ensure that your operating and other expenses are not excessive. You can win at the gross profit level and still lose the battle if your operating expenses are too high.

The pretax profit ratio is used rather than the net income ratio because industry averages are always calculated on a pretax basis. This is because some forms of business, such as partnerships and S corporations, do not pay any tax. After-tax comparisons would therefore be misleading. But it can still be useful to calculate the net income ratio for your own purposes.

When used in concert, the gross profit and pretax profit ratios are effective measures of profitability.

SERVICE COMPANY PROFITABILITY ANALYSIS

Service businesses sometimes use a slightly different income statement format:

Revenue
<u>– Operating expenses</u>

Operating profit
<u>+ / – Other income/expense</u>

Pretax profit
<u>– Income tax</u>

Net income

These income statements do not reflect cost of goods sold, since service businesses do not have goods to sell. But as you can see, they do not reflect gross profit either. This portrayal is incorrect. The correct way for service businesses to present their income statement is as follows:

Revenue
<u>– Direct expenses</u>

Gross profit
<u>– Indirect expenses</u>

Operating profit
<u>+ / – Other income/expense</u>

Profit before tax
<u>– Income tax</u>

Net income

Direct expenses are those that are directly related to producing revenue; they are similar in concept to cost of goods sold. Examples include direct labor, materials, and miscellaneous other direct expenses (travel, meals, and so on).

When direct expenses are subtracted from revenue, the result is gross profit. With this format, a service business can measure and track the gross profit ratio in the same fashion as other types of business.

Since this is not a common format, it may be difficult to obtain industry averages for the gross profit ratio. In the absence of industry averages, service businesses should establish their own standards for the gross profit ratio using historical experience. They should measure actual results against those standards.

The gross profit ratio is just as important for a service business as for those engaged in selling a product. It is one of the tools that should be utilized to price the services the company offers.

INCOME STATEMENT ADJUSTMENTS

Some financial advisors counsel that the best strategy in a business is to make no profits at all. If there is no profit, there will be no taxes. The result of this advice is that occasionally some items get expensed through the business that are not exactly business related (travel, entertainment, club dues, etc.). There have also been times (as shocking as this may seem) when business owners have taken out a higher salary than they were actually worth.

This strategy reduces pretax profit artificially, which distorts the ratios. For this reason, it is wise to add back any such expenses or excess salary to pretax profits in order to get a true picture of the company's profitability. Always be sure, however, to first calculate the ratios using the numbers as published on your income statement so that they will be comparable to industry averages.

This book is not about how to minimize income tax. It's about how to achieve financial success, and that means maximizing, not minimizing, profit. Besides, under current tax laws the opportunities for profit manipulation are few and far between and probably not worth the effort or risk involved.

CASE STUDY: DURGAN ELECTRIC CO.

On the next page you will find income statements for Durgan Electric Co. for the periods 19X1 through 19X3. This is called a spread of the income statements.

Common Size Analysis

Just as with the balance sheets, there is another analysis of your income statements (in addition to the ratios listed earlier) that allows comparison to prior periods or to others in your industry.

Durgan Electric Co.
Income Statement Spread
($000s)

	19X1		19X2		19X3	
Sales	$5,368	100.0%	$4,750	100.0%	$4,845	100.0%
Cost of goods sold	4,123	76.8	3,657	77.0	3,755	77.5
Gross Profit	$1,245	23.2	$1,093	23.0	$1,090	22.5
Operating Expense						
Advertising	33	0.6	14	0.3	12	0.3
Bad debts	52	1.0	31	0.7	48	1.0
Depreciation	49	0.9	50	1.1	53	1.1
Equipment leases	17	0.3	16	0.3	18	0.4
Insurance	53	1.0	62	1.3	59	1.2
Legal and accounting	25	0.5	27	0.6	26	0.5
Miscellaneous	39	0.7	19	0.4	4	0.1
Office supplies	29	0.5	24	0.5	25	0.5
Rent	60	1.1	60	1.3	60	1.2
Repairs and maintenance	31	0.6	29	0.6	30	0.6
Salaries, owner	75	1.4	75	1.6	75	1.6
Salaries, other	510	9.5	453	9.5	459	9.5
Salary-related expense	100	1.9	82	1.7	88	1.8
Taxes and licenses	27	0.5	25	0.5	22	0.5
Telephone	19	0.4	20	0.4	18	0.4
Travel and entertainment	8	0.1	7	0.1	6	0.1
Vehicle expense	22	0.4	21	0.4	23	0.5
Total Operating Expense	1,149	21.4	1,015	21.4	1,026	21.2
Operating Profit	$ 96	1.8	$ 78	1.6	$ 64	1.3
Interest expense	(16)	(0.3)	(12)	(0.3)	(10)	(0.2)
Pretax Profit	$ 80	1.5	$ 66	1.4	$ 54	1.1
Income tax	(20)	(0.4)	(16)	(0.3)	(13)	(0.3)
Net Income	$ 60	1.1	$ 50	1.1	$ 41	0.8

A *common size analysis* of the income statements involves dividing all of your expenses by sales to see what each expense is as a percentage of sales.

This analysis should be done every time you produce an income statement (ideally monthly). In this fashion, you can easily see if any of your expenses are increasing as a percentage of sales. This would indicate that expenses are growing faster than sales and corrective action should be taken. Your accountant or bookkeeper should routinely provide these calculations on your income statements.

The percentage columns on the Durgan income statements reflect the common size calculations. You can make the following observations from those calculations:

1. Cost of goods sold has increased from 76.8 percent to 77.5 percent since 19X1. This may not seem like a large increase, but it is 0.7 percent of sales, which is nearly $34,000 (0.007 × $4,845,000). This is the additional gross profit that Durgan would have had if the percentage had been maintained at the 19X1 level.

2. Operating expenses have been very stable as a percentage of sales, indicating that they have not increased faster than sales.

3. Pretax profit has steadily declined as a percentage of sales. This was caused mainly by the deterioration in the gross profit percentage.

Profitability Analysis

The following are the gross profit ratios for Durgan for the last three years:

	19X1	19X2	19X3	Industry Average
Gross profit ratio	23.2%	23.0%	22.5%	24.0%

As you can see, the gross profit ratio has steadily declined. In addition, at 22.5 percent in 19X3, it is 1.5 percent below the industry average. That may not sound like much, but it is 1.5 percent of $4,845,000 (19X3 sales).

Financial Impact Analysis

The financial impact of the low gross profit ratio on profits can be calculated as follows:

$4,845,000	19X3 sales
× 0.015	Variance to industry
$ 73,000	Additional gross profit if gross profit ratio is 1.5% higher

Durgan would have $73,000 more in gross profit if the gross profit ratio were 24 percent instead of 22.5 percent. This is fairly significant, because *all* of it would have been reflected in the pretax profit for 19X3. This would have made pretax profit $127,000 instead of $54,000, an increase of almost 135 percent. In other words, if the gross profit ratio could be increased by 1.5 percent, pretax profit would increase 135 percent!

Reasons for low gross profit ratio. It is not possible to determine why the gross profit ratio is low without further investigation, but it will be due to one or more of the following reasons:

1. Poor pricing.
2. Poor purchasing.
3. Geographical influences (the industry average is national).
4. Poor inventory control (slippage, spoilage, obsolescence).
5. Bookkeeping errors.
6. Poor manufacturing productivity.
7. Poor product mix (some products have higher margins than others).

Bob Durgan should be very concerned about the slippage in the gross profit ratio, since it has had quite a negative impact on pretax profits.

The following are the pretax profit ratios for the three-year time period:

	19X1	19X2	19X3	Industry Average
Pretax profit ratio	1.5%	1.4%	1.1%	2.1%

The trend of this ratio is not good, and the pretax profit ratio is 1 percent lower than the industry average in 19X3. Profitability is poor and declining for Durgan. There are two main reasons for this, decline in sales and decline in the gross profit ratio. Every effort should be made to build sales and profit margins in this business.

SUMMARY

The gross profit ratio and the pretax profit ratio are used to measure the profitability of your business. A very small increase or decrease in the gross profit ratio can have a tremendous impact on your bottom line.

Performing a financial impact analysis on your income statement allows you to determine whether you are having problems managing cost of goods sold or operating expenses (or both).

This profitability analysis should be carried out for service businesses in the same fashion. If you own or operate a service business, make every effort to determine your direct expenses and ask your bookkeeper or accountant to reformat your income statement accordingly. Then write an article for your trade publication suggesting that all of your fellow owners do likewise. Eventually, everyone will do a better job of pricing their services, and the result of having this information will be improved margins and profitability.

The income statement analysis for Durgan Electric indicates that the gross profit ratio is considerably lower than the industry average, which had a very negative impact on pretax profit.

The next chapter will look at some elements that combine accounts from both the balance sheet and the income statement in order to measure the operating performance of your business.

Chapter Five

Operating Performance Analysis

T he last chapter discussed how to analyze the income statement and measure profitability. In this chapter, accounts from both balance sheet and income statement will be used to analyze operating performance.

Your primary objective as a business owner is to take a collection of assets, financed with either debt (money from creditors) or equity (money from owners), and generate profits. The ratios described in this chapter measure how well you are performing this job. This analysis is also referred to as asset/liability management, and the reader should not be dismayed or confused if other terminology is used or if these ratios are lumped in with others in different categories.

OPERATING PERFORMANCE RATIOS

The following nine ratios are used to measure operating performance:

1. Sales to assets.
2. Return on assets.
3. Return on equity.
4. Inventory turnover.
5. Inventory turn (days).
6. Accounts receivable turnover.
7. Accounts receivable collection period (days).
8. Accounts payable turnover.
9. Accounts payable period (days).

Sales to Assets

The sales to assets ratio is calculated as follows:

$$\frac{\text{Sales}}{\text{Total assets}}$$

This ratio measures the dollar amount of sales generated per dollar of assets employed. A low ratio indicates that the business has excess assets in relation to the volume of sales. The solution is to either increase sales or reduce assets. A ratio of 3.97 to 1 would mean that there was $3.97 in sales for every $1.00 of total assets.

Return on Assets

The return on assets ratio is calculated as follows:

$$\frac{\text{Pretax profit}}{\text{Total assets}}$$

The primary objective of any business owner is to take a collection of assets and make money with them. This ratio is a way to quantify how well this task is being accomplished. A ratio of 10.0 percent would mean that the business generated $0.10 in pretax profit for every $1.00 of assets employed.

Return on Equity

Return on equity is calculated as follows:

$$\frac{\text{Pretax profit}}{\text{Equity}}$$

Business owners often have a considerable sum of money invested (equity) in their businesses, and a satisfactory return should be derived from this investment. There are alternative investments where these funds might be employed, many with less risk. It is important to measure the return being generated in the business to see how favorably it compares to returns available elsewhere. A ratio of 15.0 percent would indicate that the business generated $0.15 in pretax profit for every $1.00 in equity employed.

Inventory Turn

Inventory turnover and inventory turn days are calculated as follows:

$$\frac{\text{Cost of goods sold}}{\text{Inventory}} = \text{Inventory turnover}$$

$$\frac{\text{Days in period}}{\text{Inventory turnover}} = \text{Inventory turn days}$$

If the cost of goods sold is for one year, then 365 is the number of days used in the formula. If it is a six-month period, use 180 days. An inventory turnover ratio of 6.0 would indicate that the inventory turns over six times per year, or every 61 days (365 ÷ 6).

Inventory is an asset that should be managed or monitored on a regular basis. A business should not have any more money tied up in inventory than is absolutely necessary. Excess inventory causes excess interest, insurance, storage, spoilage, obsolescence, shrinkage, and the like, all of which has a negative impact on profitability.

The major automobile manufacturers and other firms currently increase inventory turnover with a system called just-in-time inventory. An engine is delivered at the exact time it is needed on the assembly line. The goal is to have the absolute minimum amount of inventory on hand in order to minimize carrying costs and maximize profitability.

Accounts Receivable Turn

Accounts receivable turnover and accounts receivable collection period (days) ratios are calculated as follows:

$$\frac{\text{Sales}}{\text{Accounts receivable}} = \text{Accounts receivable turnover}$$

$$\frac{\text{Days in period}}{\text{Accounts receivable turnover}} = \text{Collection period days}$$

Accounts receivable is another asset that should be managed on a regular basis, and the amount invested in this asset should be the absolute minimum needed. Excess accounts receivable costs money in interest expense if financed with bank debt and can lead to increased bad debt expense, thus reducing profits.

An accounts receivable turnover ratio of 8.0 would indicate that the accounts receivable turn over eight times per year, or every 45 days (365 ÷ 8).

Accounts receivable and inventory are called *trading assets*. The following diagram shows how these trading assets interact with sales.

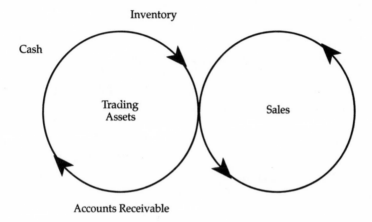

You can see that it is advantageous to spin the trading asset wheel as fast as possible, since every time it revolves it produces cash. You increase turnover by either maintaining your inventory and accounts receivable levels constant while increasing sales or reducing inventories and accounts receivable for the same level of sales.

Turnover ratios reveal the optimal relationship of inventory and accounts receivable to sales or costs of goods sold in your business. Calculating the turnover ratios on a regular basis will help you maintain the appropriate levels of these assets.

Frequent aging of accounts receivable is also helpful in this analysis. To age receivables, separate them into categories based on their due date:

Age	Expressed as
0 to 30 days	$ and %
31 to 60 days	$ and %
61 to 90 days	$ and %
over 90 days	$ and %

The objective is to have the minimum dollar and percentage amount in the over-30-day categories. Constant monitoring will facilitate this process. An aging analysis is particularly important to your banker, because banks typically will not lend money against accounts receivable that are over 60 (or 90) days old.

Accounts Payable Turn

Accounts payable turnover and accounts payable period (days) ratios are calculated as follows:

$$\frac{\text{Cost of goods sold}}{\text{Accounts payable}} = \text{Accounts payable turnover}$$

$$\frac{\text{Days in period}}{\text{Accounts payable turnover}} = \text{Account payable period days}$$

Accounts payable should be paid when due. Excess trade payables can lead to restriction of credit or placement of the business on cash on delivery (COD) status. Either event can put a severe crimp in the ability of the business to operate smoothly and efficiently.

An accounts payable turnover ratio of 10.0 would mean that the accounts payable turn over 10 times per year, or every 37 days (365 ÷ 10).

CASE STUDY: DURGAN ELECTRIC CO.

Following are the sales to assets ratios for Durgan for the last three years:

	19X1	19X2	19X3	Industry Average
Sales to assets	3.00	2.71	2.80	3.20

The sales to assets ratio has declined somewhat over the period and is lower than the industry average. This is not too surprising in light of the decline in sales. The ratio of 2.80 in 19X3 means that Durgan generated $2.80 in sales for every $1.00 of assets employed in the business.

Following are the return on assets ratios for Durgan for the last three years:

	19X1	19X2	19X3	Industry Average
Return on assets	4.5%	3.8%	3.1%	6.7%

Return on assets has declined steadily as a result of the decline in profits. It is substantially below the industry average of 6.7 percent. The ratio of 3.1% in 19X3 indicates that the company generated only $0.031 in pretax profits for every $1.00 of assets employed in the business.

Following are the return on equity ratios for Durgan for the last three years:

	19X1	19X2	19X3	Industry Average
Return on equity	7.2%	5.7%	4.5%	15.5%

Return on equity has also steadily declined over the last three years. It is substantially below the industry average of 15.5 percent. The ratio of 4.5 percent in 19X3 indicates that the company generated only $0.045 in pretax profits for every $1.00 of equity employed in the business.

While our prior analysis indicated that this was not a particularly risky business, a return of 4.5 percent is still very low. If there are no prospects for increasing profits, Bob Durgan should consider selling the business and investing his funds elsewhere.

Following are the inventory turnover and inventory turn days ratios for the last three years:

	19X1	19X2	19X3	Industry Average
Inventory turnover	6.1x	6.3x	5.9x	5.8x
Inventory turn days	60 days	58 days	62 days	63 days

Inventory turnover and inventory turn days ratios have remained relatively constant over the last three years and are very close to industry averages. The ratio of 5.9 in 19X3 indicates that the inventory is turning over 5.9 times per year, or every 62 days.

Following are the accounts receivable and collection period days ratios for the last three years:

	19X1	19X2	19X3	Industry Average
Accounts receivable turnover	8.3x	8.3x	10.3x	7.8x
Collection period	44 days	44 days	35 days	47 days

Accounts receivable turnover and the collection period days are both excellent in 19X3; they have improved over prior years. A ratio of 10.3 in 19X3 indicates that the accounts receivable are turning over 10.3 times per year, or every 35 days. This is substantially better than the industry average of 7.8 times and 47 days. This may indicate that Durgan is restricting sales by selling to only the most creditworthy customers. Loosening up somewhat on the credit standards of the company may increase sales. This is only speculation at this point; it should be examined very carefully before the credit policy is changed at all.

Following are the accounts payable turnover and accounts payable period days for the last three years:

	19X1	19X2	19X3	Industry Average
Accounts payable turnover	9.1x	10.2x	9.9x	8.9x
Payment period	40 days	36 days	37 days	41 days

Accounts payable turnover and the payment period have been very constant over the years and are slightly better than the industry averages. A ratio of 9.6 in 19X3 indicates that the accounts payable turn over 9.6 times per year, or every 38 days. This is slightly better than the industry average of 41 days, which is not surprising, since our analysis of the balance sheet indicated excellent liquidity (ability to pay bills).

Durgan's Financial Condition

The following is a summary of the financial condition of Durgan Electric:

1. Liquidity and safety are both excellent and improving. The balance sheet is very solid.
2. Profitability is poor and declining, in both margins and dollars. The income statement is weak.
3. Operating performance is spotty. Sales to assets, return on assets, and return on equity are all poor and declining. The inventory turnover, accounts receivable turnover, and accounts payable turnover ratios are all good.

The strong balance sheets, combined with the deteriorating income statements, are typical of a company in the plunder phase of business. Durgan is in a state of decline and should use some of its cash and apparent borrowing power to expand and revitalize the business. Expanding may increase risk somewhat, but the alternative may very well be that the company ultimately begins to lose money and is eventually liquidated.

The plunder phase is a tough phase to be in. The situation may be satisfactorily resolved only when, or if, the owner decides it is time to step down and let the next generation take over.

SUMMARY

This chapter has discussed nine ratios that measure operating performance. When combined with the other five ratios outlined in chapters 3 and 4, they will give you a pretty clear picture of the financial condition of your business. The ratios should be calculated for the last five years so that trends can be observed, and they should be compared to industry averages when available.

The next chapter will discuss one of the most important aspects of effective financial management, cash flow analysis.

Chapter Six

Cash Flow Analysis

M ost business owners are driven to increase sales and profits. If some sales are good, then more are better. The objective is to make lots of money and get to the thunder phase of business as quickly as possible. Unfortunately, this myopic focus on sales and profits often excludes the very thing that is most important to a business: cash flow.

You pay your bills, your payroll, your taxes, and your bank loans with cash. It could be argued that the only entity that cares how much you make in profits is the IRS. So why this intense focus on profits? There are several reasons for it.

1. It seems intuitively correct that the more money you make, the more money you will have.

2. Cash flow is not well understood. If you ask five experienced financial analysts their definition of cash flow, you may get five different answers.

3. Your accountant has only recently supplied you with a statement of cash flow so that you can effectively track your cash flow on a regular basis.

A concentration on profits might be okay if cash flow could always be equated with profits. Regrettably, this is seldom the case. In fact, it is quite possible to have great profits and terrible cash flow. There can even be an inverse relationship between profits and cash flow. Of course, it is important for you to be profitable. But good cash flow is just as important to the long-term success of your business.

Factors from both the income statement and the balance sheet generate cash flow in your business. These factors can be either positive or negative, as the following diagram shows.

FINANCIAL STATEMENT CASH FLOW FACTORS

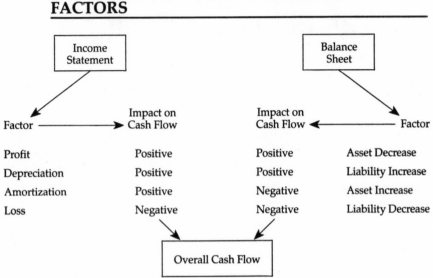

Factor	Impact on Cash Flow	Impact on Cash Flow	Factor
Profit	Positive	Positive	Asset Decrease
Depreciation	Positive	Positive	Liability Increase
Amortization	Positive	Negative	Asset Increase
Loss	Negative	Negative	Liability Decrease

Positive Cash Flow Factors

Positive contributions to cash flow from the income statement include profits, depreciation, and amortization. The emphasis here is on the word *contribution*. Profits do not equal cash flow; they merely contribute to it.

Depreciation and amortization are noncash expense items on the income statement. You do not write a check for depreciation. This is why, from a cash flow standpoint, it is added back to profits. Cash flow is generated from the balance sheet when assets go down or liabilities go up. If you sell equipment or decrease accounts receivable, that supplies cash. If you get a bank loan or increase accounts payable, that also supplies cash.

Negative Cash Flow Factors

Losses (after being reduced by depreciation or amortization) are a negative contribution to cash flow from the income statement. Cash flow is reduced by the balance sheet when assets go up or liabilities go down. If you buy equipment or increase accounts receivable or inventory, that takes cash. Similarly, a decrease in any liability has a negative impact on cash.

As you study the diagram carefully, you will begin to see why an increase in profits may cause a decrease in cash flow. As sales and profits go up, so do assets like accounts receivable, inventory, and equipment. When assets go *up*, cash goes *down*. This is why there may be an inverse relationship between profits and cash flow.

DEFINITIONS OF CASH FLOW

The statement of cash flow, as provided to you by your CPA, is separated into three categories of cash flow: operating cash flow, investing cash flow, and financing cash flow. If you understand and monitor these three types of cash flow in your business, it is not likely that you will ever have a cash flow problem.

Operating Cash Flow

Operating cash flow is cash flow generated from operations. It consists of profits, depreciation, and changes in your operating assets:

Net profit after tax
+ Depreciation/amortization
+ / − Changes in accounts receivable
+ / − Changes in inventory
+ / − Changes in prepaid expenses and other noncash current assets
+ / − Changes in accounts payable
+ / − Changes in accrued expenses
+ / − Changes in other noncash current liabilities
= Operating cash flow

How much operating cash flow is enough? Simply having a lot of operating cash flow is not necessarily desirable. For example, not paying your accounts payable would generate a lot of operating cash flow, but this would cause other problems.

Operating cash flow needs to be analyzed within the bigger picture of the financial condition of your business. A rapid growth in sales is likely to cause a large increase in both accounts receivable and inventory and therefore result in negative operating cash flow. If the balance sheet ratios are solid and reflect good liquidity and safety, then you can probably withstand negative operating cash flow without adverse consequences to the business.

One principle can be stated here with absolute certainty. You cannot have negative operating cash flow every year. Sooner or later you must generate positive operating cash flow, or you cannot survive.

Investing Cash Flow

Investing cash flow consists of changes in marketable securities, investments, and fixed assets:

Changes in marketable securities
+ / − Changes in long-term investments
+ / − Changes in gross fixed assets
+ / − Nonrecurring gains or losses
+ / − Changes in other nonoperating assets

=   Investing cash flow

Marketable securities consist of investments in publicly traded securities and are not considered to be part of the normal operating assets of a business, so changes in this account are not included in operating cash flow. Long-term investments include such things as investments in subsidiaries or other businesses. Nonrecurring gains or losses usually involve the sale of a fixed asset. They may also be related to a gain or loss in a legal action.

For most businesses, the majority of changes in investing cash flow will involve increases or decreases in gross fixed assets. If sales are increasing, these assets are likely to increase, thus causing negative investing cash flow.

Financing Cash Flow

Financing cash flow is divided into two main categories, debt and equity. Debt cash flow is either short or long term. Equity cash flow is in the form of either dividends paid or additional capital supplied by owners.

Changes in short-term bank debt
+ / − Changes in long-term bank debt
+ / − Changes in shareholder debt
−   Dividends paid
+   Capital investment
_____
=   Financing cash flow

For most businesses, financing cash flow will come from additional bank debt. Not many businesses pay dividends (since they are not deductible for tax purposes), and typical business owners do not have a pile of cash that they can invest in the business (and even if they did, their spouse might forbid it).

The total cash flow of the business is the combination of the three basic types of cash flow:

Operating cash flow
+ / − Investing cash flow
+ / − Financing cash flow
_____
=   Total cash flow

ANALYZING CASH FLOW

Cash flow is not particularly easy to analyze. There are no standard ratios for it. And what seems intuitively to make sense about cash flow may not be true. As an example, positive operating cash flow is not always good, for at least two reasons: The business may be declining and liquidating its operating assets, or the business may have delayed paying its accounts payable. Either of these factors will produce positive operating cash flow, but both are harmful to the success of the business.

By the same token, negative operating cash flow is not always bad, because growth in sales and profits can cause an increase in operating assets, which will cause negative operating cash flow. This may be beneficial to the business.

What can be stated with some degree of certainty are the following two principles:

1. Over time, operating cash flow must be enough to at least provide for the down payment requirements of investing

cash flow and the short-term debt payments in financing cash flow.

2. Over time, negative cash flow before financing (operating cash flow plus or minus investing cash flow) *will not work.*

At some point, absent additional equity capital, the business simply must produce positive cash flow before financing cash flow. Otherwise debt (in the absence of additional equity) will increase beyond safe limits and creditors will demand payment (usually at an awkward time).

CASH FLOW RATIO ANALYSIS

Due to the lack of cash flow ratios in general practice, it is necessary to design some for analysis purposes. Four ratios will help you analyze the cash flow of your business: cash flow to profit, cash flow debt coverage, cash return on assets, and cash return on equity. Since industry averages do not exist, your task is to calculate these ratios for your business over several years and then develop management standards you believe are appropriate. (This is exactly what you should do with the other ratios also.)

Cash Flow to Profit

This ratio is calculated as follows:

Operating cash flow

Pretax profit

Expressed as a percentage, this ratio will tell you the amount of your pretax profit that is actually cash. A ratio of 0.255 indicates that operating cash flow is 25.5 percent of your pretax profit. What this *should* be is not obvious, but you might aim for at least the income tax rate for your business. If you pay 30 percent income tax on your profits, then it would be nice to have 30 percent of your profits in *cash* so that you can make this payment. The IRS has a funny attitude about requiring cash, not profits, in payment of income taxes.

Cash Flow Debt Coverage

This ratio is calculated as follows:

$$\frac{\text{Interest-bearing debt}}{\text{Cash flow before financing}}$$

Cash flow before financing is the combination of operating cash flow and investing cash flow. Expressed in years, this ratio will tell you how long, based on current cash flow, it will take to pay off all of your interest-bearing debt.

A ratio of 7.5, for example, indicates that it will take 7.5 years to pay off all of your existing debt, based on the current level of cash flow. If the longest loan maturity you have is only five years, then your current level of cash flow will not provide for repayment of your debt. If this condition is expected to continue, it would be wise to make other provisions or attempt to renegotiate the loans.

Cash Return on Assets

This ratio is calculated as follows:

$$\frac{\text{Operating cash flow}}{\text{Total assets}}$$

This ratio is similar to the return on assets ratio described earlier. A ratio of 0.085 indicates a cash flow return on assets of 8.5 percent.

Cash Return on Equity

This ratio is calculated as follows:

$$\frac{\text{Operating cash flow}}{\text{Equity}}$$

This ratio is similar to the return on equity ratio described earlier. A ratio of 0.155 indicates a cash flow return on equity of 15.5 percent.

Calculating these ratios is one thing. Understanding what they *should* be in your business is something else. The absence of industry averages means that you are going to have to figure this out for yourself, through experience.

That's the bad news. The good news is that you're going to feel pretty good about yourself when you actually understand what these cash flow ratios should be in your business. You will find yourself in such an elite minority of business owners that your friends and colleagues will flock to you for advice. You will be sought out for speeches at association meetings, and you will probably be able to sell the business and live on your honorariums (a much easier life).

CASE STUDY: DURGAN ELECTRIC CO.

The following page reflects the cash flow statement for the last three years for Durgan Electric. Only two years are reflected, 19X2 and 19X3, because the statement of cash flow is a period statement. It reflects changes in financial condition from one period to the next. Thus, only two columns can be generated from three periods: the changes from 19X1 to 19X2 (labeled 19X2) and the changes from 19X2 to 19X3 (labeled 19X3).

Operating Cash Flow

You will note that operating cash flow of $166,000 in 19X2 and $157,000 in 19X3 bear little relationship to the net income for those years. This is primarily due to the reduction in accounts receivable in both years and the reduction in inventory in 19X2. Since sales and profits are generally declining, this positive operating cash flow is not necessarily good.

Investing Cash Flow

The investing cash flow of ($62,000) in 19X2 and ($45,000) in 19X3 was caused by an increase in gross fixed assets.

Financing Cash Flow

Durgan has no short-term bank debt, so the only impact on financing cash flow was caused by changes in long-term debt.

Durgan Electric Co.
Statement of Cash Flow
($000s)

	Year	
Account Item	*19X2*	*19X3*
Net income after tax	$ 50	$ 41
Depreciation and amortization	50	53
Accounts receivable	80	100
Inventory	96	(56)
Prepaid expenses	(1)	(2)
Accounts payable	(92)	22
Accrued expenses	(17)	(1)
Operating Cash Flow (OCF)	$166	$157
Gross fixed assets	(62)	(45)
Investing Cash Flow (ICF)	$ (62)	$ (45)
Cash Flow before Financing	104	112
Long-term bank debt	22	(85)
Financing Cash Flow (FCF)	$ 22	$ (85)
Overall Cash Flow	**$126**	**$ 27**
Beginning cash	194	320
+/− Overall cash flow	126	27
Ending cash	320	347

Overall Cash Flow

Overall cash flow totaled $153,000 for the two years, compared to only $91,000 in net income after tax. Again, you do not see any particular relationship between income and cash flow.

Cash Flow Ratios

Following are the cash flow to profit ratios for the two-year period. The ratio of 290.7 percent in 19X3 indicates that operating cash flow is almost three times pretax profit.

	19X2	*19X3*	*Industry Average*
Cash flow to profit	251.5%	290.7%	N/A

Following are the cash flow debt coverage ratios for the two-year period. The ratio of 1.1 in 19X3 indicates that Durgan can pay off all interest-bearing debt in 1.1 years, based on current cash flow.

	19X2	19X3	Industry Average
Cash flow debt coverage	2.0 years	1.1 years	N/A

Following are the cash flow return on asset ratios for the two-year period. Durgan is generating a 9.1 percent cash flow return on assets.

	19X2	19X3	Industry Average
Cash flow return on assets	9.5%	9.1%	N/A

Following are the cash flow return on equity ratios for the two-year period. Durgan is generating a 13 percent cash flow return on equity.

	19X2	19X3	Industry Average
Cash flow return on equity	14.3%	13.0%	N/A

Cash flow for Durgan appears to be excellent. Remember that this is the same company that had poor and declining profitability. This combination of good cash flow and poor profitability is fairly common for a company in the plunder phase. The business is, in effect, in a liquidation mode.

Durgan's Ratio Analysis Summary

The following page contains a summary of all of the ratios for Durgan.

- Liquidity, as reflected by the current and quick ratios, is excellent and improving over the three-year period 19X1–X3.

Durgan Electric Co.
Ratio Analysis

	19X1	19X2	19X3	Industry Average
Liquidity				
Current ratio	3.12	3.89	3.65	1.95
Quick ratio	1.73	2.34	2.04	0.90
Safety				
Debt to equity ratio	0.61	0.51	0.44	1.30
Profitability				
Gross profit ratio	23.2%	23.0%	22.5%	24.0%
Pretax profit ratio	1.5%	1.4%	1.1%	2.1%
Operating Performance				
Sales to assets	3.00	2.71	2.80	3.20
Return on assets	4.5%	3.8%	3.1%	6.7%
Return on equity	7.2%	5.7%	4.5%	15.5%
Inventory turnover	6.1x	6.3x	5.9x	5.8x
Inventory turn days	60 days	58 days	62 days	63 days
Accounts receivable turnover	8.3x	8.3x	10.3x	7.8x
Collection period	44 days	44 days	35 days	47 days
Accounts payable turnover	9.1x	10.2x	9.9x	8.9x
Payable days	40 days	36 days	37 days	41 days
Cash Flow				
Cash flow to profit	N/A	251.5%	290.7%	N/A
Cash flow debt coverage	N/A	2.0 years	1.1 years	N/A
Cash return on assets	N/A	9.5%	9.1%	N/A
Cash return on equity	N/A	14.3%	13.0%	N/A

- Safety, as reflected by the debt to equity ratio, is excellent and improving. The balance sheets are very strong.
- Profitability, as reflected by the gross profit and pretax profit ratios, is poor and declining.
- Operating performance is mixed. The turnover ratios are excellent, but the other ratios are poor and declining.
- Cash flow has been very good, which has allowed the company to reduce debt over the period.

It appears that Durgan Electric Co. is squarely in the plunder phase of business. While certain financial aspects of the company look good, the business is actually in a state of decline, and management should make every attempt to build both sales and profitability in the years ahead.

The next chapter will take a look at the company after this has been accomplished.

Chapter Seven

Durgan Electric Co.:
The Next Generation

W hen confronted with the analysis in the prior chapters, Bob Durgan decided to retire and let his son Mark take over the business. He was tired of working so hard for so little, and he could see the wisdom of letting younger blood take over.

This decision was somewhat overdue from Mark's standpoint, and he promptly made some changes in the business in order to build sales. All but one sales rep was fired, and young and aggressive reps were recruited from the competition.

Mark made a serious attempt in the next three years to build sales and increase market share. The results of his efforts are reflected in the income statements, balance sheets, statements of cash flow, and ratios on the following pages. As you can see, sales increased to $11,681,000 in 19X6. This represents a compound growth rate of 34 percent per year based on 19X3 sales. Better yet, operating profit increased fourfold, from $64,000 in 19X3 to $245,000 in 19X6. This represents tremendous improvement, and Mark is very pleased with himself.

PROBLEMS

Cash flow, however, is not quite so smashing. Operating cash flow has totaled ($1,376,000) over the three-year period. When added to investing cash flow of ($1,067,000), cash flow before financing is a whopping ($2,443,000)! It appears that cash flow gets worse as income goes up.

Durgan Electric Co.
Income Statement Spread
($000s)

	19X4		19X5		19X6	
Sales	$6,555	100.0%	$8,850	100.0%	$11,681	100.0%
Cost of goods sold	5,087	77.6	6,903	78.0	9,088	77.8
Gross Profit	1,468	22.4	1,947	22.0	2,593	22.2
Depreciation	68	1.0	97	1.1	140	1.2
Other operating expense	1,289	19.7	1,682	19.0	2,208	18.9
Total Operating Expense	1,357	20.7	1,779	20.1	2,348	20.1
Operating Profit	$ 111	1.7	$ 168	1.9	$ 245	2.1
Interest expense	(30)	(0.5)	(69)	(0.8)	(125)	(1.1)
Pretax Profit	$ 81	1.2	$ 99	1.1	$ 120	1.0
Income tax	(20)	(0.3)	(25)	(0.3)	(30)	(0.3)
Net Income	$ 61	0.9	$ 74	0.8	$ 90	0.8

You now know, of course, why this is happening. You could have predicted it. The rapid increase in sales caused an increase in accounts receivable, inventory, and equipment, which caused negative cash flow.

The next section assesses the financial condition of Durgan after three years of Mark's leadership.

Liquidity

Liquidity, as measured by the current and quick ratios, is now poor and declining.

The current ratio of 1.32 in 19X6 means that there is $1.32 in current assets to pay each $1.00 in current liabilities. The quick ratio of 0.55 in 19X6 means that there is $0.55 in cash and accounts receivable to pay every $1.00 of current liabilities. Both ratios are declining and are substantially below industry averages.

Durgan Electric Co.
Balance Sheet Spread
($000s)

Assets	19X4		19X5		19X6	
Cash	$ 105	4.4%	$ 51	1.4%	$ 30	0.6%
Accounts receivable	762	31.9	1,196	33.0	1,693	32.8
Inventory	978	41.0	1,534	42.4	2,392	46.3
Prepaid expenses	15	0.6	21	0.6	28	0.5
Total Current Assets	$1,860	77.9	$2,802	77.4	$4,143	80.2
Leasehold improvements	118	5.0	151	4.2	191	3.6
Furniture and equipment	1,183	49.5	1,538	42.4	1,845	35.7
Gross Fixed Assets	1,301	54.5	1,689	46.6	2,036	39.3
Less: Depreciation	(773)	(32.4)	(870)	(24.0)	(1,010)	(19.5)
Net Fixed Assets	528	22.1	819	22.6	1,026	19.8
Total Assets	**$2,388**	**100.0**	**$3,621**	**100.0**	**$5,169**	**100.0**
Liabilities						
Notes payable, bank	$ 195	8.2	$ 921	25.4	$1,659	32.1
Accounts payable, trade	628	26.3	874	24.1	1,443	27.9
Accrued expenses	27	1.1	37	1.0	48	0.9
Total Current Liabilities	$ 850	35.6	$1,832	50.5	$3,150	60.9
Long-Term Debt	273	11.4	450	12.5	590	11.4
Total Liabilities	**$1,123**	**47.0**	**$2,282**	**63.0**	**$3,740**	**72.3**
Equity						
Stock	75	3.1	75	2.1	75	1.5
Retained earnings	1,190	49.8	1,264	34.9	1,354	26.2
Total Equity	**$1,265**	**52.9**	**$1,339**	**37.0**	**$1,429**	**27.7**
Total Liabilities and Equity	**$2,388**	**100.0**	**$3,621**	**100.0**	**$5,169**	**100.0**

Durgan Electric Co.
Statement of Cash Flow
($000s)

Account Item	19X4	19X5	19X6
		Year	
Net income after tax	$ 61	$ 74	$ 90
Depreciation and amortization	68	97	140
Accounts receivable	(292)	(434)	(497)
Inventory	(342)	(556)	(858)
Prepaid expenses	(4)	(6)	(7)
Accounts payable	247	246	569
Accrued expenses	7	10	11
Operating Cash Flow (OCF)	$(255)	$(569)	$(552)
Gross fixed assets	(332)	(388)	(347)
Investing Cash Flow (ICF)	$(332)	$(388)	$(347)
Cash flow before financing	(587)	(957)	(899)
Short-term bank debt	195	726	738
Long-term bank debt	150	177	140
Financing Cash Flow (FCF)	$ 345	$ 903	$ 878
Overall Cash Flow	$(242)	$ (54)	$ (21)
Beginning cash	347	105	51
+/− Overall cash flow	(242)	(54)	(21)
Ending cash	$ 105	$ 51	$ 30

Safety

Safety, as measured by the debt to equity ratio, is marginal and declining. The ratio of 2.62 in 19X6 means that there is $2.62 in debt for every $1.00 in equity. This is more than twice the industry average of 1.30, and reflects considerably more risk.

Profitability

Profitability, as measured by the gross profit and pretax profit ratios, is poor and declining. This is caused primarily by the increased interest expense caused by the increased debt.

Durgan Electric Co.
Ratio Analysis

	19X4	19X5	19X6	Industry Average
Liquidity				
Current ratio	2.19	1.53	1.32	1.95
Quick ratio	1.02	0.68	0.55	0.90
Safety				
Debt to equity ratio	0.89	1.70	2.62	1.30
Profitability				
Gross profit margin	22.4%	22.0%	22.2%	24.0%
Pretax profit margin	1.2%	1.1%	1.0%	2.1%
Operating Performance				
Sales to assets	2.74	2.44	2.26	3.20
Return on assets	3.4%	2.7%	2.3%	6.7%
Return on equity	6.4%	7.4%	8.4%	15.5%
Inventory turnover	5.2x	4.5x	3.8x	5.8x
Inventory turn days	70 days	81 days	96 days	63 days
Accounts receivable turnover	8.6x	7.4x	6.9x	7.8x
Collection period	42 days	49 days	53 days	47 days
Accounts payable turnover	8.1x	7.9x	6.3x	8.9x
Payable days	45 days	46 days	58 days	41 days
Cash Flow				
Cash flow to profit	Negative	Negative	Negative	N/A
Cash flow debt coverage	Negative	Negative	Negative	N/A
Cash return on assets	Negative	Negative	Negative	N/A
Cash return on equity	Negative	Negative	Negative	N/A

The gross profit ratio has declined 0.3 percent since 19X3 (from 22.5 to 22.2 percent). This may not sound like much, but it represents lost profits of $35,000 ($11,681,000 × 0.003). An increase in the gross profit ratio of just 0.3 percent would increase pretax profits over 29 percent (from $120,000 to $155,000). This is evidence of the tremendous importance of the gross profit ratio.

Operating Performance

Mark has saved the worst for last. All of the operating performance ratios, except return on equity, have deteriorated, and all are substantially below industry averages. The company now has more accounts receivable, inventory, and accounts payable than is warranted based on the level of sales.

Cash Flow Ratios

None of the cash flow ratios can be calculated because they are all negative and therefore meaningless. In just three short years, Mark Durgan has taken an extremely safe (if somewhat boring) company to the brink of collapse. This has happened primarily because Mark has not monitored the ratios on a regular basis and has instead focused on sales and profits.

The business has grown too fast and outstripped the available capital. It is growing broke. Previously in the plunder phase, the company is now squarely in the blunder phase, and Mark is making his share of blunders.

SOLUTIONS

The problems are easy to spot from the ratio analysis, and so are the solutions. Mark should take the following corrective action to get the company back on a sound financial footing:

1. Increase the gross profit ratio to at least the industry average of 24 percent by a combination of altering product mix, pricing better, and taking advantage of trade discounts.

2. Increase the inventory turnover to at least 5.8 times per year. This would mean reducing inventory to $1,567,000. Calculate this by dividing the cost of goods sold in 19X6, $9,088,000 (from the income statement), by the industry average turnover of 5.8. The result—$1,567,000—is the amount of inventory the company should have if it turns 5.8 times per year. This would be a reduction of $825,000 ($2,392,000 − $1,567,000).

3. Increase the <u>accounts receivable</u> turnover to at least 7.8 times per year. This would mean reducing accounts receivable to $1,498,000. Calculate this by dividing the sales in 19X6, $11,681,000, by 7.8 (the industry average). The result—$1,498,000—is the amount of inventory the company should have it if turns 7.8 times per year. This would be a reduction of $195,000 ($1,693,000 − $1,498,000).

4. Increase the <u>accounts payable turnover</u> to at least 8.9 times per year. This would mean reducing accounts payable to $1,021,000. Calculate this by dividing cost of goods sold in 19X6, $9,088,000, by the industry average of 8.9. The result—$1,021,000—is what the company should have in accounts payable if it turns them 8.9 times per year. This would be a reduction of $422,000 ($1,443,000 − $1,021,000).

5. Use the cash generated from reducing inventory and <u>accounts receivable</u> to reduce short-term bank debt. Calculate this by adding the reduction in inventory to the reduction in accounts receivable ($825,000 + $195,000 = $1,020,000), then subtracting the amount used to reduce accounts payable ($1,020,000 − $422,000 = $598,000).

6. Develop a financial plan for the next three years that reflects better financial management and an improvement in the financial ratios.

Implementing the first five solutions would restate the financial statements for 19X6 as follows:

Sales	$11,681,000 [1]
Gross profit	2,803,000 [2]
Operating expenses	2,348,000 [1]
Operating profit	455,000
Interest expense	(125,000)[1]
Pretax Profit	$ 330,000
Cash	$ 30,000 [1]
Accounts receivable	1,498,000 [3]
Inventory	1,532,000 [4]
Prepaid expenses	28,000 [1]
Current assets	$ 3,088,000
Net fixed assets	1,026,000 [1]
Total Assets	$ 4,114,000

(continued)

Notes payable (bank)	$ 1,049,000 [5]
Accounts payable	998,000 [6]
Accrued expenses	48,000 [1]
Current liabilities	$ 2,095,000
Long-term debt	590,000 [1]
Total Liabilities	2,685,000
Equity	1,429,000 [1]
Total Liabilities and Equity	$ 4,114,000

[1]Actual for 19X6.

[2]Based on gross profit ratio of 24%.

[3]Based on accounts receivable turnover of 7.8x.

[4]Based on inventory turnover of 5.8x.

[5]This is the resulting number that balances the balance sheet after all of the other adjustments have been made.

[6]Based on accounts payable turnover of 8.9x.

If Mark had managed the company properly in 19X6, the ratios would have been as follows:

	19X6 Actual	19X6 Revised	Industry Average
Liquidity			
Current ratio	1.32	1.47	1.95
Quick ratio	0.55	0.73	0.90
Safety			
Debt to equity ratio	2.62	1.88	1.30
Profitability			
Gross profit ratio	22.2%	24.0%	24.0%
Pretax profit ratio	1.0%	2.8%	2.1%
Operating Performance			
Sales to assets	2.26	2.84	3.20
Return on assets	2.3%	8.0%	6.7%
Return on equity	8.4%	23.1%	15.5%
Inventory turnover	3.8x	5.8x	5.8x
Accounts receivable turnover	6.9x	7.8x	7.8x
Accounts payable turnover	6.3x	8.9x	8.9x

Liquidity and safety are not yet as good as industry averages, but they are at very tolerable levels. Profitability, with just a 1.8 percent increase in the gross profit ratio, is very good. The operating performance ratios are all excellent. Cash flow is still going to be negative, but Mark can correct this by slowing the rate of growth in sales in future years. Revised financial statements for 19X6 appear on the next few pages.

These solutions are all doable, and even a minimal amount of attention to these ratios would have avoided the problems in the first place. Mark is a salesman, not a financial analyst, and he did very well in building sales. But that was not enough—it almost never is.

SUMMARY

Every business owner should pay attention to the financial side of the business on a regular basis. The ratios measuring liquidity, safety, profitability, operating performance, and cash flow are the *minimum* that should be calculated.

Use these 18 ratios. Get to the point where you really understand them. Success is not guaranteed, but at least you will be doing the right things for the right reasons at the right time, and probably avoiding problems before they have a chance to develop.

Additional Ratios

The ratios presented in this book that measure liquidity, safety, profitability, operating performance, and cash flow are generic to all types of businesses. Obviously, if you have no inventory or accounts receivable, you can skip those ratios. The rest of them will still apply. In addition to these 18 ratios, you may find a few other key relationships that are important in measuring success in your business. Be careful not to add too many ratios, however. Too much information can lead to confusion. A good rule is never to calculate a ratio unless you know what it means. There is no end to the number of ratios that a well-programmed computer will calculate, but more is not necessarily better.

Durgan Electric Co.
Income Statement 19X6
($000s)

	19X6 Actual		19X6 Revised	
Sales	$11,681	100.0%	$11,681	100.0%
Cost of goods sold	9,088	77.8	8,878	76.0
Gross Profit	2,593	22.2	2,803	24.0
Depreciation	140	1.2	140	1.2
Other operating expense	2,208	18.9	2,208	18.9
Total Operating Expense	2,348	20.1	2,348	20.1
Operating Profit	$ 245	2.1	$ 455	3.9
Interest expense	(125)	(1.1)	(125)	(1.1)
Pretax Profit	$ 120	1.0	$ 330	2.8
Income tax	(30)	(0.3)	(83)	(0.7)
Net Income	$ 90	0.8	$ 247	2.1

Think about ratios in your business it might be useful to track in addition to those presented. Search out those areas that are critical to the success of your business and monitor them carefully. You can then dig deeper into a particular problem area if appropriate.

Limitations of Ratio Analysis

Ratio analysis is at the heart of the historical analysis process and it is important that business owners use and apply it on a regular basis. It is the best way to ensure that you are on the right track from a financial standpoint, and not headed for trouble.

It is not, however, all that needs to be done from a management standpoint. Poor ratios are not really the problem, they are the symptoms of problems. People, products, and services are what make a business successful, and it is not possible to quantify their quality or competence into ratios.

There is no substitute for good management, and unfortunately entrepreneurs who start businesses are often not experienced or competent managers. Moreover, they are not particularly

Durgan Electric Co.
Balance Sheet 19X6
($000s)

	19X6 Actual		19X6 Revised	
Assets				
Cash	$ 30	0.6%	$ 30	0.7%
Accounts receivable	1,693	32.8	1,498	36.4
Inventory	2,392	46.3	1,532	37.2
Prepaid expenses	28	0.5	28	0.7
Total Current Assets	$4,143	80.2	$3,088	75.0
Leasehold improvements	191	3.6	191	4.6
Furniture and equipment	1,845	35.7	1,845	44.9
Gross Fixed Assets	2,036	39.3	2,036	49.5
Less: Depreciation	(1,010)	(19.5)	(1,010)	(24.5)
Net Fixed Assets	1,026	19.8	1,026	25.0
Total Assets	**$5,169**	**100.0**	**$4,114**	**100.0**
Liabilities				
Notes payable, bank	$1,659	32.1	$1,049	25.5
Accounts payable, trade	1,443	27.9	998	24.3
Accrued expenses	48	0.9	48	1.2
Total Current Liabilities	$3,150	60.9	$2,095	51.0
Long-Term Debt	590	11.4	590	14.3
Total Liabilities	**$3,740**	**72.3**	**$2,685**	**65.3**
Equity				
Stock	75	1.5	75	1.8
Retained earnings	1,354	26.2	1,354	32.9
Total Equity	**$1,429**	**27.7**	**$1,429**	**34.7**
Total Liabilities and Equity	**$5,169**	**100.0**	**$4,114**	**100.0**

interested in or well suited for management. Entrepreneurs are action oriented, hands-on people. "If you want it done well you have to do it yourself" is the common plea. Management, however, involves getting things done through other people.

Durgan Electric Co.
Ratio Analysis

	19X6 Actual	19X6 Revised	Industry Average
Liquidity			
Current ratio	1.32	1.47	1.95
Quick ratio .	0.55	0.73	0.90
Safety			
Debt to equity ratio	2.62	1.88	1.30
Profitability			
Gross profit margin	22.2%	24.0%	24.0%
Pretax profit margin	1.0%	2.8%	2.1%
Operating Performance			
Sales to assets	2.26	2.84	3.20
Return on assets	2.3%	8.0%	6.7%
Return on equity	8.4%	23.1%	15.5%
Inventory turnover	3.8x	5.8x	5.8x
Inventory turn days	96 days	63 days	63 days
Accounts receivable turnover	6.9x	7.8x	7.8x
Collection period	53 days	47 days	47 days
Accounts payable turnover	6.3x	8.9x	8.9x
Payable days	58 days	41 days	41 days

Planning and delegation are integral aspects of effective management.

Managing a business requires different skills than starting a business. Technical expertise is necessary in the wonder phase, and management expertise is necessary in the blunder and thunder phases. Resolve to either learn and apply effective management skills or find someone else to be your general manager.

Ratio analysis enables you to spot areas that need attention, and effective management is necessary to take corrective action.

The discussion of the historical analysis process has now been completed. While you can't change the past, you can certainly learn from it. The calculation of key ratios provides a solid foundation for your financial plan. With this information, you can make

TABLE 7–1
Financial Impact Formulas

Total Liability Impact:

Equity × Target debt to equity = Target liabilities
Actual liabilities − Target liabilities = Financial impact

Gross Profit Impact:

Sales × Target gross profit margin = Target gross profit
Target gross profit − Actual gross profit = Financial impact

Pretax Profit Impact:

Sales × Target pretax profit margin = Target pretax profit
Target pretax profit − Actual pretax profit = Financial impact

Sales Impact:

Total assets × Target sales to assets = Target sales
Target sales − Actual sales = Financial impact

Total Asset Impact:

Sales ÷ Target sales to assets = Target total assets
Actual total assets − Target total assets = Financial impact

Inventory Impact:

Cost of goods sold ÷ Target inventory turnover = Target inventory
Actual inventory − Target inventory = Financial impact

Accounts Receivable Impact:

Sales ÷ Target accounts receivable turnover = Target accounts receivable
Actual accounts receivable − Target accounts receivable = Financial impact

Accounts Payable Impact:

Cost of goods sold ÷ Target accounts payable turnover = Target accounts
payable
Actual accounts payable − Target accounts payable = Financial impact

---

intelligent decisions about your financial projections in the next few years.

To make sure you follow the historical analysis process, let's review the steps:

1. Spread your financial statements for the last five years.

2. Calculate the ratios as discussed in chapters 3 through 6.

3. Examine the trends and compare to industry averages, if available. Also compare your performance to your established goals.

4. Identify the problems, if any, that the ratio analysis has revealed.

5. Calculate the financial impact of the problems you have identified. (Refer to the financial impact formulas at the end of this chapter.)

6. List your solutions and begin to take corrective action.

The next chapter introduces the subject of planning for the future.

Chapter Eight

Introduction to Planning

"**I** f you don't know where you're going, you may wind up somewhere else." "Fail to plan, plan to fail." You pick the cliché. They all apply. Operating without a business plan is like navigating without a compass; you just never know what you might run in to.

RESISTANCE TO PLANNING

Most business owners do not like to plan. As entrepreneurs they tend to be action oriented, and planning is not something that comes naturally. The task immediately before them is what gets their attention.

Management versus Operations

Planning is part of management work, and business owners are not often well suited for this type of work. They tend to be more comfortable with the operational side of the business—what the company does—than with pushing paper around in an office. They see management as the boring desk work part of the business, and it isn't that much fun.

Lack of Knowledge

Not knowing how or what to plan is a difficult barrier to overcome without a fair amount of effort. Help is certainly available. This book describes how to generate a financial plan, and there are many books available about how to write a business plan.

A detailed description of the entire business planning process is beyond the scope of this book, but the last chapter contains an outline for a business plan and checklists of key questions to answer in the areas of management, marketing, and finance.

Lack of Time

When asked why they do not plan, business owners will most frequently answer, "I'm already working 10 or 12 hours a day, 6 and 7 days a week struggling to be successful in this business. When am I supposed to find time to plan?"

Well, no one said owning a business was easy. Planning is hard work, but it doesn't take time, it *saves* time. Instead of answering the same questions over and over, you answer them once. With a plan, you become *proactive* instead of reactive. Everything is more orderly and efficient. Time invested at the outset in the form of a business plan pays great dividends in time saved in the long run.

Fear

Fear of the unknown. Fear of the future. Fear of being held accountable. Fear of not making it. If you put a plan down on paper, others can see it. They will know if you don't achieve it. They may be critical of your performance. Who needs this? Better not to commit yourself in the first place. That way, whatever happens, you can say it was what you expected.

Results of Not Planning

Unfortunately, a lack of planning is often the cause of serious problems or outright failure. Poor management and planning are estimated to account for over 90 percent of the business failures that occur.

Promise yourself that you will learn how to develop a business plan for your business and invest the time necessary to this process. Don't use one of these excuses as a cop-out, or you may never make it to the thunder phase!

STRATEGIC PLANNING

Effective business planning starts with a look at the big picture—the basic strategies the company should employ in the next few years. Failure to devote proper attention to this aspect of planning is akin to drifting in a boat down an unexplored river. Most of your effort is devoted to the task at hand, steering the boat away from the river banks and dangerous rocks so that it will not become damaged or stranded.

The low rumbling sound that is barely perceptible in the distance is not given much thought. Things are going pretty well at the moment, and besides, you are so busy guiding the boat that you don't really have time to think about anything else. Maybe that rumbling will go away.

But the rumbling gets progressively louder. Eventually you, the boat, and everyone in it are flung over an unseen, unplanned for—but nevertheless fatal—waterfall, onto the rocks below. Of course the waterfall was avoidable. There was ample evidence that it was there, but no one in the boat was paying attention to anything that far ahead.

Elevating your sights once in a while and taking a longer look into the future at what may affect your business helps to avoid unpleasant and possibly fatal surprises. Assessing your overall business environment at least annually allows you to set effective long-term strategies for your business.

It is often easy to miss the significance of certain signals or events in the future operating environment of your business. Many businesses were deregulated in the 1980s, for example, which caused severe disruption in industries like trucking, stock brokerage, banking, and airlines. The legislation that deregulated these industries was discussed and debated for years before it was enacted, so there was ample time for forward-thinking business owners to adapt their business strategies.

Those companies that have survived and prospered in the postderegulation environment are the ones that made the effort to assess what the new rules might be and how best to position their businesses to minimize problems and maximize opportunities.

The following diagram is a model of the strategic planning process.

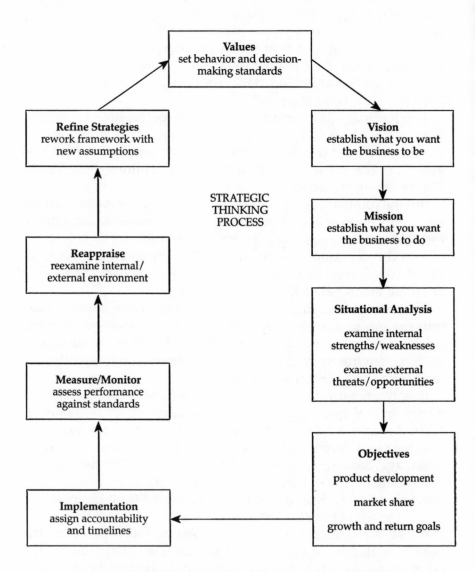

It starts with a definition of the values of the owners and moves toward the establishment of a vision and/or mission for the company.

Mission Statement

A vision or mission statement should be a concise one- or two-paragraph statement that reflects the main purpose or focus of your business. It may answer questions like:

1. Why does the business exist?
2. What do you believe in?
3. What does the business *really* do?
4. What values do the owners/employees have?

You may be surprised how difficult it is to boil the entire company down to a single statement, but it is an important part of the exercise. You may want to have key employees and selected outsiders review this statement to make sure it properly reflects the feelings and values of those who are expected to implement it.

Situational Analysis

The situational analysis involves an assessment of both the external and internal environments of the business. The formal term for this process is *environmental scanning*.

The external analysis assesses the following items:

The competition.

Legal/regulatory changes.

The economy.

Social trends.

Emerging technology.

In this exercise you are looking for *opportunities* and *threats* that could possibly have an impact on your business. Effective strategies will take advantage of the opportunities and minimize the threats.

The internal analysis assesses the following items:

Personnel capabilities.

Plant capacity.

Financial capacity.

Products/services.

Organizational structure.

In this exercise you are looking for an honest, candid assessment of the *strengths* and *weaknesses* of your business. Effective strategies will take advantage of the strengths and minimize the weaknesses.

Objectives

Setting objectives is the next step. They are often set in the following areas:

Growth rate for sales or profits.

Dollar amount of sales or profits.

Return on assets or investment.

Market share.

Product development.

Objectives should be specific, realistic, flexible, measurable, and well documented. Specific tasks and timetables should be clearly spelled out to avoid misunderstandings as to who is responsible for what and in what time frame.

Implementation

People need to be assigned specific tasks. Time lines must be established. Careful monitoring should take place to make sure plans, goals, and objectives are on track. This is a key phase of the process. Do not succumb to the temptation to simply put the plan on the shelf and forget about it. Nothing will happen, and you will have wasted a lot of time and effort.

Reappraisal

The only constant in your life is change. Nothing remains the same. At least once a year, take a look at your strengths, weaknesses, opportunities, and threats. Reassess the overall direction of your business. Refine your mission, goals, and objectives. Make sure to involve the key people in your company. Keep them informed as to where you are going and what you are trying to do.

BENEFITS OF PLANNING

There are many benefits of planning. They include:

1. Encouraging management to consider and evaluate basic company policies.
2. Encouraging management to look ahead to consider conditions that are likely to prevail outside the company.
3. Promoting a team concept within the key management of the company.
4. Planning for the most effective and economical use of labor, materials, facilities, and capital.
5. Promoting understanding throughout the company of the problems faced by each department or division.
6. Serving as a means to evaluate progress or lack of it toward stated goals.
7. Providing a commitment to a plan of action.
8. Instilling in management at all levels the habit of carefully considering all factors before making a final decision.
9. Avoiding or minimizing costly mistakes or errors in judgment.
10. Maintaining the focus on the stated mission and objectives of the company rather than various sideshow distractions..

FINANCIAL PLAN

The financial plan consists of the following:

1. Long-range projected income statements.
2. Long-range projected balance sheets.
3. Long-range projected cash flow.

4. Long-range projected financial ratios.
5. Short-range projected income statements.
6. Short-range projected cash budget.

Chapters 10 through 13 contain a complete description of how to develop long- and short-range financial plans.

Time Frame

The time frame for making these projections will vary depending on the industry and the individual business. For some industries, like aircraft manufacturers, it is necessary to plan at least 10 years ahead. For others, such as small contractors or retailers, it may be difficult to see more than six months to a year ahead.

Most companies should make financial forecasts for a three-year time period. Each year more information is available, and the forecast can then be revised appropriately and pushed out another year.

Trendline Forecasts

A trendline forecast is based strictly on what has already happened. It assumes that the business will operate in the future exactly as it has in the past, which is not a bad place to begin the financial plan.

A trendline forecast will dramatically point out what areas, if any, need attention in the next few years. Of course, if the historical analysis has been done thoroughly, these areas should not come as any surprise. They should have already been well diagnosed and solutions implemented. A trendline forecast should merely reinforce what has already been determined.

CASE STUDY: DURGAN ELECTRIC CO.

On the following pages you will find projected income statements, balance sheets, statements of cash flow, and ratios for Durgan Electric.

These are trendline projections that assume that the company will operate in the future exactly as it has in the past. Growth rates, profit margins, and turnover ratios have been projected based on 19X6 results.

Trendline Projected Income Statements

As you can see, by 19X9 sales are projected to be $26,859,000 and operating profit is $640,000. It is hard not to get excited about these results. Sales and profits have grown magnificently!

By now, however, you know that you cannot tell much by simply looking at the numbers. We need to look at some *key relationships* before getting too excited. Nevertheless, it is interesting to contemplate owning and operating a business this size.

Trendline Projected Balance Sheets

Durgan Electric Co.
Trendline Income Statement Forecast
($000s)

	19X7		19X8		19X9	
Sales	$15,418	100.0%	$20,349	100.0%	$26,859	100.0%
Cost of goods sold	11,996	77.8	15,832	77.8	20,896	77.8
Gross Profit	3,422	22.2	4,517	22.2	5,963	22.2
Depreciation	301	2.0	419	2.1	553	2.1
Other operating expense	2,782	18.0	3,631	17.8	4,770	17.7
Total Operating Expense	3,083	20.0	4,050	19.9	5,323	19.8
Operating Profit	$ 339	2.2	$ 467	2.3	$ 640	2.4
Interest expense	(228)	(1.5)	(320)	(1.6)	(439)	(1.6)
Pretax Profit	$ 111	0.7	$ 147	0.7	$ 201	0.8
Income tax	(28)	(0.2)	(37)	(0.2)	(50)	(0.2)
Net Income	$ 83	0.5	$ 110	0.5	$ 151	0.6

Durgan Electric Co.
Trendline Balance Sheet Forecast
($000s)

	19X7		19X8		19X9	
Assets						
Cash	$ 31	0.5%	$ 41	0.5%	$ 54	0.5%
Accounts receivable	2,236	32.7	2,951	32.7	3,895	32.7
Inventory	3,161	46.3	4,172	46.3	5,506	46.3
Prepaid expenses	31	0.5	41	0.5	54	0.5
Total Current Assets	$5,459	80.0	$7,205	80.0	$9,509	80.0
Leasehold improvements	247	3.6	326	3.6	430	3.6
Furniture and equipment	2,436	35.7	3,215	35.7	4,244	35.7
Gross Fixed Assets	2,683	39.3	3,541	39.3	4,674	39.3
Less: Depreciation	(1,311)	(19.3)	(1,730)	(19.3)	(2,283)	(19.3)
Net Fixed Assets	1,372	20.0	1,811	20.0	2,391	20.0
Total Assets	**$6,831**	**100.0**	**$9,016**	**100.0**	**$11,900**	**100.0**
Liabilities						
Notes payable, bank	$2,559	37.5	$3,752	41.7	$5,319	44.7
Accounts payable, trade	1,912	28.0	2,523	28.0	3,331	28.0
Accrued expenses	62	0.9	81	0.9	107	0.9
Total Current Liabilities	$4,533	66.4	$6,356	70.6	$8,757	73.6
Long-Term Debt	786	11.5	1,038	11.5	1,370	11.5
Total Liabilities	**$5,319**	**77.9**	**$7,394**	**82.1**	**$10,127**	**85.1**
Equity						
Stock	75	1.1	75	0.8	75	0.6
Retained earnings	1,437	21.0	1,547	17.1	1,698	14.3
Total Equity	**$1,512**	**22.1**	**$1,622**	**17.9**	**$1,773**	**14.9**
Total Liabilities and Equity	**$6,831**	**100.0**	**$9,016**	**100.0**	**$11,900**	**100.0**

Durgan Electric Co.
Trendline Statement of Cash Flow Forecast
($000s)

	Year		
Account Item	*19X7*	*19X8*	*19X9*
Net income after tax	$ 83	$ 110	$ 151
Depreciation and amortization	301	419	553
Accounts receivable	(543)	(715)	(944)
Inventory	(769)	(1,011)	(1,334)
Prepaid expense	(3)	(10)	(13)
Accounts payable	469	611	808
Accrued expenses	14	19	26
Operating Cash Flow (OCF)	$ (448)	$ (577)	$ (753)
Gross fixed assets	(647)	(858)	(1,133)
Investing Cash Flow (ICF)	$ (647)	$ (858)	$(1,133)
Cash flow before financing	(1,095)	(1,435)	(1,886)
Short-term bank debt	900	1,193	1,567
Long-term bank debt	196	252	332
Financing Cash Flow (FCF)	$ 1,096	$ 1,445	$ 1,899
Overall Cash Flow	$ 1	$ 10	$ 13
Beginning cash	30	31	41
+/− Overall cash flow	1	10	13
Ending cash	$ 31	$ 41	$ 54

Already our enthusiasm is diminished. We can see that short-term bank debt has grown to over $5.3 million. Holy default! That's a lot of money. The increase in sales caused an increase in assets, which caused negative cash flow, which caused the increase in debt.

Trendline Projected Cash Flow

Operating cash flow totals ($1,778,000) for the three-year period, and cash flow before financing is a whopping ($4,416,000). This has been caused by an increase in accounts receivable, inventory, and equipment.

Durgan Electric Co.
Trendline Ratio Analysis Forecast

	19X7	19X8	19X9	Industry Average
Liquidity				
Current ratio	1.20	1.13	1.09	1.95
Quick ratio	0.50	0.47	0.45	0.90
Safety				
Debt to equity ratio	3.52	4.56	5.71	1.30
Profitability				
Gross profit margin	22.2%	22.2%	22.2%	24.0%
Pretax profit margin	0.7%	0.7%	0.8%	2.1%
Operating Performance				
Sales to assets	2.26	2.26	2.26	3.20
Return on assets	1.6%	1.6%	1.7%	6.7%
Return on equity	7.3%	9.1%	11.3%	15.5%
Inventory turnover	3.8x	3.8x	3.8x	5.8x
Inventory turn days	96 days	96 days	96 days	63 days
Accounts receivable turnover	6.9x	6.9x	6.9x	7.8x
Collection period	53 days	53 days	53 days	47 days
Accounts payable turnover	6.3x	6.3x	6.3x	8.9x
Payable days	58 days	58 days	58 days	41 days
Cash Flow				
Cash flow to profit	Negative	Negative	Negative	N/A
Cash flow debt coverage	Negative	Negative	Negative	N/A
Cash return on assets	Negative	Negative	Negative	N/A
Cash return on equity	Negative	Negative	Negative	N/A

Trendline Projected Ratios

It should be no surprise to see that every ratio has deteriorated badly. Sales, profits, assets, and equity have all gone up dramatically, and the company is in the tank. This is dramatic proof that you cannot tell anything by looking only at the numbers and neglecting key relationships.

The trendline forecast reflects that the company cannot continue to operate in the future as it has in the past. Corrective action must be taken on the gross profit ratio and the turnover ratios, and the growth rate in sales must be reduced somewhat.

SUMMARY

Most business owners do not like to plan and find any number of excuses to put it off. The phone is always ringing, and it is easy to be consumed by the multitude of tasks at hand. But planning is well worth the time involved. Your very existence may depend upon it.

Managing a growing (blunder phase) company is particularly challenging; the next chapter will describe this process.

Chapter Nine

Growth Management

I f some is good, more is better. More sales and profits are better than fewer sales and profits, right? If only it were so.

In order for high growth not to be a problem, it needs to be managed carefully. You need to understand the financial dynamics of growth in your business and make sure that you do not become overextended.

FINANCIAL DYNAMICS OF GROWTH

Growth in sales causes an increase in assets. If sales double, accounts receivable and inventory are likely to double as well. The money for the increase in assets must come from one or more of the following sources:

- Profits.
- New equity capital.
- New debt.

To the extent that profits provide enough money, the business is said to be financing itself on an internal basis. Unfortunately, most businesses operate on a fairly low net profit margin, and profits by themselves are almost never enough to pay for all of the new assets required. It is also usually the case that most business owners do not have access to huge amounts of equity capital, either their own or from other sources.

That leaves new debt as the most likely source of financing the growth in the business. As debt increases, the debt to equity ratio (and therefore risk) increases. Credit lines become stretched to the limit, payments are postponed, creditors get mad, and eventually lawyers get into the act. Bankruptcy is just around the corner. It's called growing broke.

The amount of assets caused by sales depends on the rate of growth in sales, as illustrated in the following diagram.

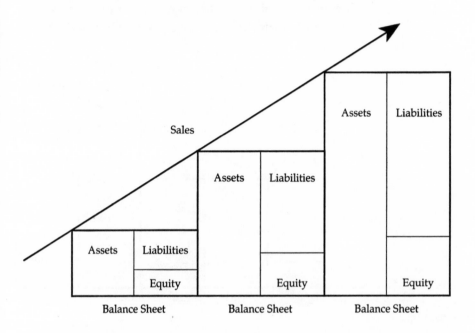

As you can see, growth in sales causes a growth in assets. Equity grows by the amount of net income (assuming no dividends are paid), which is usually a very small percentage of sales.

In this diagram, liabilities are growing faster than equity. This causes the debt to equity ratio to increase and the safety of the business to decline. In other words, as the business experiences high growth in sales and net income, it becomes more risky (as measured by the debt to equity ratio).

High growth in sales and net income may cause significant financial problems for a business. If it is carried to an extreme, you can literally grow yourself into bankruptcy. This is why your banker is sometimes in the position of asking you to reduce your rate of growth, even though building sales as rapidly as possible is your primary objective.

Reducing the rate of growth in sales does seem counterintuitive. If some sales are good, then aren't more better? But growth in sales needs to be managed very carefully from a financial standpoint. The following diagram illustrates a slower rate of growth (a less steep sales line), and you can see that the relationship between liabilities and equity remains the same. Therefore risk is not increasing.

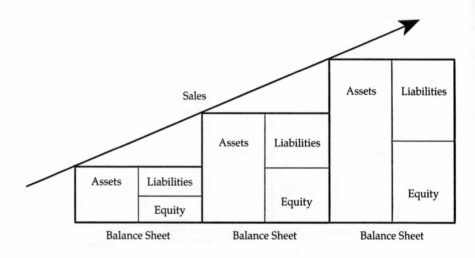

SUSTAINABLE GROWTH RATE FORMULA

Fortunately, you can calculate the rate of growth in sales your business can sustain without increasing the debt to equity ratio. The formula for calculating the sustainable growth rate for a business to maintain a constant debt to equity ratio follows:

$$\text{Sustainable growth rate} = \frac{\text{Net income percentage} \times (1 + \text{Debt to equity ratio})}{\text{Asset percentage} - [\text{Net income percentage} \times (1 + \text{Debt to equity ratio})]}$$

In this formula, net income percentage is net income divided by sales, and asset percentage is total assets divided by sales. The debt to equity ratio is total liabilities divided by equity.

CASE STUDY: DURGAN ELECTRIC CO.

The next page contains the actual and revised balance sheets for Durgan Electric for 19X6. These are identical to those in Chapter 7, except that a column labeled "% of Sales" has been added. Assets and liabilities have been divided by sales to determine their relationship to sales. These percentages can then be used in calculating a sustainable growth rate for the business.

For actual 19X6, assets totaled 44.3 percent of sales. The net income ratio was 0.8 percent (net income divided by sales), and the debt to equity ratio was 2.62. These numbers can be substituted into the formula as follows:

$$\text{Sustainable growth rate} = \frac{\text{Net income percentage} \times (1 + \text{Debt to equity ratio})}{\text{Asset percentage} - [\text{Net income percentage} \times (1 + \text{Debt to equity ratio})]}$$

$$= \frac{0.008 \times (1 + 2.62)}{0.443 - [0.008 \times (1 + 2.62)]}$$

$$= \frac{0.029}{0.443 - 0.029}$$

$$= \frac{0.029}{0.414}$$

$$= 0.07 = 7.0\%$$

This means that Durgan's sales can grow at a rate of 7 percent per year and maintain the debt to equity ratio of 2.62. If sales grow faster than 7 percent, the debt to equity ratio (and therefore the risk) will increase. If sales grow less than 7 percent, the debt to equity ratio will go down, and the company will become safer.

A maximum growth rate of 7 percent is bad news for Mark Durgan, because he feels the company can easily grow 15 percent per year for the next three years. There is hope, however. In Chapter 7 we reconstructed what the 19X6 income statement and balance sheet would have looked like if Mark had done a little better job managing profits, accounts receivable, and inventory. The revised

Durgan Electric Co.
Balance Sheet 19X6
($000s)

Assets	19X6 Actual $	19X6 Actual % of Sales	19X6 Revised $	19X6 Revised % of Sales
Cash	30	0.3	30	0.3
Accounts receivable	1,693	14.5	1,498	12.8
Inventory	2,392	20.5	1,532	13.1
Prepaid expenses	28	0.2	28	0.2
Total Current Assets	$4,143		$3,088	
Leasehold improvements	191		191	
Furniture and equipment	1,845		1,845	
Gross Fixed Assets	2,036	17.4	2,036	17.4
Less: Depreciation	(1,010)		(1,010)	
Net Fixed Assets	1,026	8.8	1,026	8.8
Total Assets	**$5,169**	**44.3**	**$4,114**	**35.2**
Liabilities				
Notes payable, bank	$1,659		$1,049	
Accounts payable, trade	1,443	12.4	998	8.5
Accrued expenses	48	0.4	48	0.4
Total Current Liabilities	$3,150		$2,095	
Long-Term Debt	590	5.1	590	5.1
Total Liabilities	**$3,740**		**$2,685**	
Equity				
Stock	75		75	
Retained earnings	1,354		1,354	
Total Equity	**$1,429**		**$1,429**	
Total Liabilities and Equity	**$5,169**		**$4,114**	

balance sheet reflects an asset percentage of 35.2 percent. Utilizing the revised net income percentage of 2.1 percent, the new sustainable growth rate can be calculated as follows:

$$\text{Sustainable growth rate} = \frac{\text{Net income percentage} \times (1 + \text{Debt to equity ratio})}{\text{Asset percentage} - [\text{Net income percentage} \times (1 + \text{Debt to equity ratio})]}$$

$$= \frac{0.021 \times (1 + 2.62)}{0.352 - [0.021 \times (1 + 2.62)]}$$

$$= \frac{0.076}{0.352 - 0.076}$$

$$= \frac{0.076}{0.276}$$

$$= 0.275 = 27.5\%$$

The sustainable growth rate of 27.5 percent is good news for Mark. If Mark makes the necessary changes in profitability and asset management, the company can grow at 15 percent per year for the next three years and the debt to equity ratio will go *down*, because the company will be growing at less than the sustainable growth rate.

STRATEGIES FOR MANAGING GROWTH

There are three key strategies to employ in order to grow as fast as possible.

1. Minimize your asset percentage.
2. Maximize profit margins.
3. Maximize equity.

Minimize Your Asset Percentage

A high turnover of accounts receivable and inventory will have the effect of reducing the asset percentage. The amount of accounts receivable and inventory should be the minimum necessary to sustain the level of sales. The purchase of fixed assets should also be minimized. The cash down payment required for these assets takes precious cash that is needed elsewhere in the business. Consider leasing fixed assets, even if it's a little more expensive in the form of higher interest rates. If fixed assets are purchased, finance them over as long a term as possible. This will minimize annual cash outflow and increase the company's ability to grow.

Maximize Profit Margins

It is important to get the highest profit dollars for any given level of sales, at both the gross profit and net income levels. High profit margins will increase the sustainable growth rate.

Maximize Equity

In a high-growth business, every dime of earnings should be reinvested. There is often a strong temptation to take out big bonuses when the company starts to make a lot of money; resist this temptation vigorously.

SUMMARY

Growth can be desirable, but it needs to be managed very carefully. This chapter introduced the concept of sustainable growth rate, the rate at which sales can grow without an increase in the debt to equity ratio. This is a very important calculation for a fast-growing company.

If you find yourself in the high growth phase, make sure you understand the financial dynamics of growth in your business. You do not want to grow broke.

The next chapter discusses long-range forecasting techniques for the income statements.

Chapter Ten

Income Statement Projections

U p to this point, this book has described the historical financial analysis process and discussed the financial dynamics of growth. The next step in the financial management process is the long-range plan.

FORECASTING SALES

Long-range financial planning starts with a projection of the income statements, and the first step in that process is to forecast sales. A number of relevant factors need to be taken into account in this exercise.

The status of the economy (global/national/local).
The status of the industry.
Historical sales trends.
Competition.
Market size and share.
Financial resources.
Human resources.
Physical resources.
Anticipated changes in technology.
The regulatory environment.
Product/raw material availability.
Customer preferences/social trends.
Management and employee input.

There are other factors, such as interest rates, population growth, government spending, and housing starts, that may affect any particular business. The important thing is to consider carefully all of the relevant factors that affect your business in order to make an informed and realistic forecast of sales.

CALCULATING GROSS PROFITS AND OTHER NUMBERS

Once sales have been forecasted, the gross profit is calculated based on a percentage of sales. This percentage should reflect the historical performance of the company as well as the goals and objectives of management. If you have established standards within your company for the gross profit ratio, then determine the amount of gross profit by applying that percentage to the forecasted sales. These standards need to be realistic and take into account pricing pressures in the marketplace in order to be meaningful.

If there are several divisions or branches of your company, the gross profit should be forecasted for each division based on that division's gross profit ratio and then summed for the whole company.

Calculate the cost of goods sold by subtracting the gross profit from sales. Cost of goods sold are costs directly related to generating sales, such as direct labor, raw materials, and freight.

Operating expenses should be projected either individually on a line-by-line basis or as a percentage of sales. Operating expenses are those *not* directly related to producing sales—rent, advertising, legal services, accounting, travel and entertainment, and administrative salaries.

Other income and expense are usually forecasted on the basis of historical experience. These are items of income or expense that are not considered to be either cost of goods sold or operating. Examples are interest, gain or loss on the sale of assets, and other nonrecurring items.

CASE STUDY: DURGAN ELECTRIC CO.

In the prior chapter, we determined that 27.5 percent is the sustainable growth rate for Durgan, based on the reconstructed financial statements for 19X6. Further, Mark Durgan felt that the company could easily grow at 15 percent per year for the next three years. He made this projection after carefully considering all of the pertinent factors listed above.

Mark is going to increase the gross profit ratio to at least 24 percent in the next three years with a combination of better pricing, better purchasing, and a slightly different product mix strategy. Expenses are assumed to increase at the same rate as sales, or 15 percent. This is a conservative assumption, and Mark believes he can actually do better than that if he monitors and controls expenses carefully over the period.

With these assumptions, as illustrated on the next page, net income will grow from $90,000 in 19X6 to $377,000 in 19X9. Ambitious, but management considers it doable.

SUMMARY

Most business owners have a fairly good intuitive feeling for future sales and profits, at least for one year. There is a natural reluctance, however, to commit this forecast to paper, where people can see it and know if you fail to achieve it. Who needs this hassle? Isn't the projection just as good if it is in your head? The answer is most certainly not.

Your employees want to help you achieve your goals, and they therefore need to be aware of what they are. Better yet, they should participate in the planning process. Nothing builds commitment like involvement.

In addition, projection of the balance sheets, cash flow, and financial ratios depends on the projected income statements. All of this needs to be *written down* and then consulted frequently during the year. This lets both you and your employees assess the progress toward your financial goals.

Durgan Electric Co.
Income Statement Forecast
($000s)

	19X7		19X8		19X9	
Sales	$13,433	100.0%	$15,448	100.0%	$17,765	100.0%
Cost of goods sold	10,209	76.0	11,740	76.0	13,501	76.0
Gross Profit	3,224	24.0	3,708	24.0	4,264	24.0
Depreciation	132	1.0	154	1.0	178	1.0
Other operating expense	2,568		2,951		3,393	
Total Operating Expense	2,700	20.1	3,105	20.1	3,571	20.1
Operating Profit	$ 524	3.9	$ 603	3.9	$ 693	3.9
Interest expense	(144)	1.1	(165)	1.1	(190)	1.1
Pretax Profit	$ 380	2.8	$ 438	2.8	$ 503	2.8
Income tax	(95)		(110)		(126)	
Net Income	$ 285	2.1	$ 328	2.1	$ 377	2.1

Furthermore, as you incorporate profit planning into your management process, you will develop a financial discipline that is helpful in running a successful business and the skill to better anticipate your future performance.

The next chapter discusses how to forecast the balance sheets.

Chapter Eleven

Balance Sheet Projections

A fter the income statements have been projected for the next three years, the next step is to project the balance sheets.

THE PERCENTAGE OF SALES METHOD

Balance sheets are forecasted using the *percentage of sales* method. The steps in this process follow.

1. Divide assets and liabilities by sales.

   This reveals the relationship of assets and liabilities to sales. You use this relationship to project future levels of assets and liabilities based on projected sales.

   Take the last few year's balance sheets and divide the assets and liabilities by sales for each year. See what the trend is, if any. If you determine that accounts receivable have been 15 percent of sales for the last four years, then it is reasonable to assume it will be 15 percent in the next few years. You can then project accounts receivable by simply multiplying projected sales by 15 percent.

   The only account (other than equity) that is *not* projected as a percentage of sales is notes payable, bank. That account is the *last* one projected, and it is used as a balancing number for the projected balance sheet (as explained in step 7).

2. Multiply the percentages in step 1 by projected sales.

   This step will determine the levels of assets and liabilities for future years.

3. Determine the new equity.

Calculate the new equity by adding net income to the equity for the prior year. This is repeated for each year.

4. Determine the new level of total liabilities and equity.

This is the same as total assets.

5. Determine the new level of total liabilities.

Determine total liabilities by subtracting the equity from the total liabilities and equity.

6. Determine the new level of current liabilities.

Calculate current liabilities by subtracting long-term liabilities from total liabilities.

7. Determine the notes payable, bank.

Finally, subtract accrued expenses and accounts payable and other current liabilities from total current liabilities to determine the required notes payable, bank (if any). This is the last number determined and is used to balance the balance sheet, to make sure that total assets equal total liabilities and equity.

CASE STUDY: DURGAN ELECTRIC CO.

The following page shows the actual and revised 19X6 balance sheet. As you can see, in 19X6 cash was 0.3 percent of sales, accounts receivable were 14.5 percent, inventory was 20.5 percent, gross fixed assets were 17.4 percent, and total assets were 44.3 percent of sales. On the liability side, accounts payable were 12.4 percent of sales, accrued expenses 0.4 percent, and long-term debt 5.1 percent.

When the balance sheet was reconstructed to reflect proper turnover ratios, the percentages for accounts receivable, inventory, and accounts payable were reduced. In addition, Mark Durgan determined that 0.5 percent of sales would be a more proper percentage for cash.

To calculate the projected levels of assets and liabilities as shown in the balance sheet forecast, multiply the appropriate percentages by the projected sales. (Be sure to convert a percentage to a decimal when performing this calculation by moving the decimal point two places to the left. That is, 12.8% equals 0.128.) As an example, calculate cash of $67,000 by multiplying

Durgan Electric Co.
Balance Sheet 19X6
($000s)

	19X6 Actual		19X6 Revised	
Assets	$	*% of Sales*	$	*% of Sales*
Cash	30	0.3	30	0.3
Accounts receivable	1,693	14.5	1,498	12.8
Inventory	2,392	20.5	1,532	13.1
Prepaid expenses	28	0.2	28	0.2
Total Current Assets	4,143		3,088	
Leasehold improvements	191		191	
Furniture and equipment	1,845		1,845	
Gross Fixed Assets	2,036	17.4	2,036	17.4
Less: Depreciation	(1,010)		(1,010)	
Net Fixed Assets	1,026	8.8	1,026	8.8
Total Assets	**5,169**	**44.3**	**4,114**	**35.2**
Liabilities				
Notes payable, bank	1,659		1,049	
Accounts payable, trade	1,443	2.4	998	8.5
Accrued expenses	48	0.4	48	0.4
Total Current Liabilities	3,150		2,095	
Long-Term Debt	590	5.1	590	5.1
Total Liabilities	**$3,740**		**$2,685**	
Equity				
Stock	75		75	
Retained earnings	1,354		1,354	
Total Equity	**$1,429**		**$1,429**	
Total Liabilities and Equity	**$5,169**		**$4,114**	

$13,433,000 by 0.005. Note that all amounts are rounded to the nearest $1,000. Very large businesses often round to the nearest $10,000.

Durgan Electric Co.
Balance Sheet Forecast
($000s)

Projected Sales	$13,433		$15,448		$17,765	
Accounts	19X7		19X8		19X9	
Assets	$	% of Sales	$	% of Sales	$	% of Sales
Cash	67	0.5	77	0.5	89	0.5
Accounts receivable	1,719	12.8	1,977	12.8	2,274	12.8
Inventory	1,760	13.1	2,024	13.1	2,327	13.1
Prepaid expenses	27	0.2	31	0.2	36	0.2
Total Current Assets	$3,573		$4,109		$4,726	
Gross Fixed Assets	2,337	17.4	2,688	17.4	3,091	17.4
Less: Depreciation	(1,142)		(1,296)		(1,474)	
Net Fixed Assets	1,195	8.9	1,392	9.0	1,617	9.1
Total Assets	**$4,768**	**35.5**	**$5,501**	**35.6**	**$6,343**	**35.7**
Liabilities						
Notes payable, bank	$1,173		$1,296		$1,437	
Accounts payable, trade	1,142	8.5	1,313	8.5	1,510	8.5
Accrued expenses	54	0.4	62	0.4	71	0.4
Total Current Liabilities	$2,369		$2,671		$3,018	
Long-Term Debt	685	5.1	788	5.1	906	5.1
Total Liabilities	**$3,054**		**$3,459**		**$3,924**	
Equity						
Stock	75		75		75	
Retained earnings	1,639		1,967		2,344	
Total Equity	**$1,714**		**$2,042**		**$2,419**	
Total Liabilities and Equity	**$4,768**		**$5,501**		**$6,343**	

		19X7	19X8	19X9
Sales projection		$13,433,000	$15,448,000	$17,765,000
Cash	0.5%	$ 67,000	$ 77,000	$ 89,000
Accounts receivable	12.8%	1,719,000	1,977,000	2,274,000
Inventory	13.1%	1,760,000	2,024,000	2,327,000
Prepaid expenses	0.2%	27,000	31,000	36,000
Gross fixed assets	17.4%	2,337,000	2,688,000	3,091,000
Accounts payable	8.5%	1,142,000	1,313,000	1,510,000
Accrued expenses	0.4%	54,000	62,000	71,000
Long-term debt	5.1%	685,000	788,000	906,000

Calculate the new equity for each year by adding the projected net income to the equity for the prior year, as follows:

	19X7	19X8	19X9
Old equity	$1,429,000	$1,714,000	$2,042,000
+ net income	+ 285,000	+ 328,000	+ 377,000
New equity	$1,714,000	$2,042,000	$2,419,000

The percentage of sales method is quick and easy but somewhat mechanical. It may be more appropriate in your business to fore-cast fixed assets based on specifically anticipated needs. The same is true for long-term debt. You should decide the best way to fore-cast these accounts based on what makes sense for your business.

SUMMARY

The steps in forecasting the new balance sheets are as follows:

1. Divide assets and liabilities by sales to determine their percentage to sales.
2. Calculate the new level of assets and liabilities by multiplying the percentages by projected sales.
3. Calculate the projected equity by adding the projected net income to the prior year's equity.

4. Use the amount of total assets for total liabilities and equity.
5. Subtract projected equity from total liabilities and equity to determine total liabilities.
6. Subtract long-term liabilities from total liabilities to determine current liabilities.
7. Subtract the projected accounts payable and accrued expenses (which were calculated using an appropriate percent of sales) from the total current liabilities to determine the notes payable, bank. This plug number is needed to balance the balance sheet.

The next chapter discusses Durgan Electric's projected cash flow and financial ratios, which will complete the long-range financial plan.

Chapter Twelve

Cash Flow and Ratio Projections

P rojecting cash flow and financial ratios is the final step in the long-range planning process after projecting the income statements and balance sheets. This is done in exactly the same way as described in the historical analysis discussed in Chapter 2.

After calculating the cash flow and ratios based on your financial statement projections, you may find that those projections don't work. This is the purpose of projections: they let you determine *in advance* if you are headed in the right direction from a financial standpoint. You may think you want to triple sales in the next few years, but this could be a big mistake if cash flow is negative and liquidity and safety deteriorate badly. The long-range financial plan is the tool that will allow you to lay out a road map to follow in the next three years. It will prevent you from getting into trouble and help to ensure your financial success.

CASE STUDY: DURGAN ELECTRIC CO.

The following pages show the income statements, balance sheets, cash flow statement, and financial ratios for Durgan Electric Co. for the next three years. The income statements were projected using the assumptions listed in Chapter 10 and the balance sheets were projected using the percentage of sales method outlined in Chapter 11. The statement of cash flow and ratios were calculated from the projected financial statements.

Durgan Electric Co.
Income Statement Forecast
($000s)

	19X7		19X8		19X9	
Sales	$13,433	100.0%	$15,448	100.0%	$17,765	100.0%
Cost of goods sold	10,209	76.0	11,740	76.0	13,501	76.0
Gross Profit	3,224	24.0	3,708	24.0	4,264	24.0
Depreciation	132	1.0	154	1.0	178	1.0
Other operating expense	2,568		2,951		3,393	
Total Operating Expense	2,700	20.1	3,105	20.1	3,571	20.1
Operating Profit	$ 524	3.9	$ 603	3.9	$ 693	3.9
Interest expense	(144)	1.1	(165)	1.1	(190)	1.1
Pretax Profit	$ 380	2.8	$ 438	2.8	$ 503	2.8
Income tax	(95)		(110)		(126)	
Net Income	$ 285	2.1	$ 328	2.1	$ 377	2.1

Durgan Electric Co.
Balance Sheet Forecast
($000s)

	19X7		19X8		19X9	
Assets						
Cash	$ 67	1.4%	$ 77	1.4%	$ 89	1.4%
Accounts receivable	1,719	36.1	1,977	36.0	2,274	35.9
Inventory	1,760	36.9	2,024	36.8	2,327	36.7
Prepaid expenses	27	0.6	31	0.6	36	0.6
Total Current Assets	$3,573	75.0	$4,109	74.8	$4,726	74.6
Gross Fixed Assets	2,337	49.0	2,688	48.9	3,091	48.7
Less: Depreciation	(1,142)	(24.0)	(1,296)	(23.7)	(1,474)	(23.3)
Net Fixed Assets	1,195	25.0	1,392	25.2	1,617	25.4
Total Assets	**$4,768**	**100.0**	**$5,501**	**100.0**	**$6,343**	**100.0**
Liabilities						
Notes payable, bank	$1,173	24.6	$1,296	23.5	$1,437	22.6
Accounts payable, trade	1,142	24.0	1,313	23.9	1,510	23.8
Accrued expenses	54	1.1	62	1.1	71	1.1
Total Current Liabilities	$2,369	49.7	$2,671	48.5	$3,018	47.5

(continued)

Durgan Electric Co.
Balance Sheet Forecast
($000s)

	19X7		19X8		19X9	
Long-Term Debt	685	14.4	788	14.3	906	14.3
Total Liabilities	**$3,054**	**64.1**	**$3,459**	**62.8**	**$3,924**	**61.8**
Equity						
Stock	75	1.5	75	1.4	75	1.2
Retained earnings	1,639	34.4	1,967	35.8	2,344	37.0
Total Equity	**$1,714**	**35.9**	**$2,042**	**37.2**	**$2,419**	**38.2**
Total Liabilities and Equity	**$4,768**	**100.0**	**$5,501**	**100.0**	**$6,343**	**100.0**

Durgan Electric Co.
Statement of Cash Flow Forecast
($000s)

	Year		
Account Item	*19X7*	*19X8*	*19X9*
Net income after tax	$ 285	$ 328	$ 377
Depreciation and amortization	132	154	178
Accounts receivable	(26)	(258)	(297)
Inventory	632	(264)	(303)
Prepaid expenses	1	(4)	(5)
Accounts payable	(301)	171	197
Accrued expenses	6	8	9
Operating Cash Flow (OCF)	$ 729	$ 135	$ 156
Gross fixed assets	(301)	(351)	(403)
Investing Cash Flow (ICF)	$(301)	$(351)	$(403)
Cash flow before financing	428	(216)	(247)
Short-term bank debt	(486)	123	141
Long-term bank debt	95	103	118
Financing Cash Flow (FCF)	$(391)	$ 226	$ 259
Overall Cash Flow	**$ 37**	**$ 10**	**$ 12**
Beginning cash	30	67	77
+ / − Overall cash flow	37	10	12
Ending cash	$ 67	$ 77	$ 89

Durgan Electric Co.
Ratio Analysis Forecast

	19X7	19X8	19X9	Industry Average
Liquidity				
Current ratio	1.51	1.54	1.57	1.95
Quick ratio	0.75	0.77	0.78	0.90
Safety				
Debt to equity ratio	1.78	1.69	1.62	1.30
Profitability				
Gross profit margin	24.0%	24.0%	24.0%	24.0%
Pretax profit margin	2.8%	2.8%	2.8%	2.1%
Operating Performance				
Sales to assets	2.82	2.81	2.80	3.20
Return on assets	8.0%	8.0%	7.9%	6.7%
Return on equity	22.2%	21.5%	20.8%	15.5%
Inventory turnover	5.8x	5.8x	5.8x	5.8x
Inventory turn days	63 days	63 days	63 days	63 days
Accounts receivable turnover	7.8x	7.8x	7.8x	7.8x
Collection period	47 days	47 days	47 days	47 days
Accounts payable turnover	8.9x	8.9x	8.9x	8.9x
Payable days	41 days	41 days	41 days	41 days
Cash Flow				
Cash flow to profit	191.8%	30.8%	31.0%	N/A
Cash flow debt coverage	4.3 years	Negative	Negative	N/A
Cash return on assets	15.3%	2.5%	2.5%	N/A
Cash return on equity	42.5%	6.6%	6.5%	N/A

Cash Flow

As you can see, operating cash flow is very positive for the three-year period. It is especially good in 19X7, due primarily to the one-time reduction of inventory of $632,000. That is due to the increase in inventory turnover from 19X6 to 19X7 and cannot be counted on in subsequent years.

Investing cash flow is negative each year due to the increase in gross fixed assets. An increase in assets causes a decrease in cash flow, and vice versa.

Cash flow before financing turns negative in 19X8 and 19X9, and this deficit must be made up with either additional equity or debt. In this case, Durgan has increased both short- and long-term debt to make up the cash flow shortfall.

Financial Ratios

Both liquidity and safety are improving over the three-year period. This means that the balance sheets are getting stronger, despite the fact that bank debt is increasing. The current, quick, and debt to equity ratios do not quite match the industry averages in 19X9, but they are well within tolerable limits, and the trend is good. If Mark can maintain these margins, profitability will be very good.

The operating performance ratios are all excellent, but this is primarily because of the assumptions used in forecasting the financial statements. It still remains for Mark to manage the assets (primarily accounts receivable and inventory) in accordance with the assumptions.

The cash flow ratios appear to be OK, but industry averages for these ratios are not available. The negative cash flow debt coverage ratio in 19X8 and 19X9 is not of great concern at this point because the trend of the debt to equity ratio is declining. The company cannot operate on a deficit cash flow basis indefinitely, however, or it will grow broke. The long-range financial plan beyond 19X9 will have to address this issue.

SUMMARY

This chapter completes the description of the long-range financial planning process. The long-range plan begins with a forecast of sales, which should use well-thought-out assumptions on the economy, markets, competition, and other key areas. The rest of the income statement is projected based on historical or desired profit margins and a line-by-line forecast of overhead expenses.

The balance sheets are forecasted utilizing the percentage of sales method. Cash flow and ratios are then calculated to determine whether or not the growth projections actually make sense from a financial standpoint.

The next step in the financial forecasting process is to forecast the first year of the long-range plan on a monthly basis. Short-range planning and seasonal cash flow projections are described in the next chapter.

Chapter Thirteen

Short-Range Projections

T he last three chapters described the long-range financial plan, which consisted of projected income statements, balance sheets, ratios, and cash flow for a three-year time period. This chapter describes the short-range financial plan, which projects the first year of the long-range plan on a monthly basis.

The short-range financial plan allows you to monitor your progress throughout the year. With a monthly income statement, you will be able to determine if you are on track for the year as far as sales and profits are concerned. If you did not learn until the end of the year that you had not attained your desired goals, it would obviously be too late to take corrective action.

The short-range financial plan also helps you determine your cash flow needs caused by any seasonal variation in your business. Specifically, you can use it to figure out (1) how much money will be required, (2) when you will need it, and (3) when you will be able to pay it back. The short-range financial plan, then, is a very important tool in managing your business during the year.

MONTHLY INCOME STATEMENTS

The first goal of the short-range financial planning process is to project next year's income statement on a monthly basis.

1. Divide monthly sales for the last several years by annual sales to determine the average percentage of sales in each month.

2. Multiply next year's projected sales by the average percentages in step one to determine monthly sales. (If your business has no seasonal pattern, simply divide your annual sales projection by 12 to calculate monthly sales.)

3. Multiply next year's projected gross profit by the monthly percentages to calculate the monthly gross profit.
4. Subtract monthly gross profit from sales to arrive at monthly cost of goods sold.
5. Distribute operating expenses monthly based on when you expect to incur them. For many businesses, operating expenses will be spread evenly throughout the year.
6. Determine monthly operating profit by subtracting operating expenses from gross profit.
7. Determine monthly pretax profit by adding or subtracting other income or other expense. These items may or may not be spread evenly throughout the year.

The result is a monthly projection of pretax profit. Since income tax is not paid monthly, this is usually as far as you need to go from a practical standpoint. (Estimated taxes are often paid quarterly, but for this example we assume they are paid in April.)

Next, you can derive a monthly cash budget based on the monthly income statements and additional assumptions about cash flow.

MONTHLY CASH BUDGET

The monthly cash budget will allow you to determine how much debt is needed during the year (if any), when the debt will be needed, and when the debt will be repaid.

Calculate the monthly cash budget as follows:

1. Project cash inflows. In order to project cash inflows, you need to answer several questions, including:
   - How much of the monthly sales will be in cash?
   - When, on average, will credit sales be collected?
   - If there is other income, when will it be collected?
2. Project cash outflows. Cash outflows depend on when you expect to pay operating expenses and accounts payable payments. You also need to project purchases of fixed assets, payment of taxes, and the like.

3. Subtract total disbursements from total cash inflow to determine monthly cash surplus or deficit.
4. Add the surplus to or subtract the deficit from the beginning cash for the month to determine the ending cash balance. The ending cash balance becomes the beginning cash balance for the next month. Carry out this process for 12 consecutive months.

The monthly cash budget determines your cash surplus or deficit on a monthly basis. The cumulative cash deficit, if any, must be covered by existing cash or short-term debt (usually referred to as a seasonal line of credit).

CASE STUDY: DURGAN ELECTRIC CO.

Based on Durgan's three-year plan from Chapter 10, 19X7 is projected as follows:

Sales	$13,433,000
Cost of goods sold	10,209,000
Gross profit	$ 3,224,000
Depreciation	132,000
Other operating expenses	2,568,000
Operating profit	$ 524,000
Other income (expense)	(144,000)
Pretax profit	$ 380,000
Income tax	(95,000)
Net income	$ 285,000

Monthly Income Statements

Sales and gross profit per month are calculated using the following monthly percentages (based on historical averages):

January	4.5%	May	14.5%	September	7.8%
February	5.3%	June	14.5%	October	5.0%
March	6.8%	July	14.5%	November	4.5%
April	7.2%	August	12.2%	December	3.2%

Monthly gross profit is subtracted from monthly sales to determine monthly cost of goods sold. Depreciation and other operating expenses are spread evenly throughout the year, at $11,000 and $214,000, respectively. Operating expenses are subtracted from gross profit to determine monthly operating profit.

Other income is zero, and other expense (interest) is $12,000 a month. This is subtracted from operating profit to determine pretax profit.

The next page shows the monthly projected income statement for 19X7, based on these assumptions.

Monthly Cash Budget

The next step is to calculate the monthly cash budget. This requires assumptions regarding the cash inflows and outflows.

Cash inflows. In this case, we assume that all sales are on a credit basis and the collection period is 60 days. So $465,000 will be collected in January from the prior November sales, and $434,000 will be collected in February from December sales. After that, collections are based on monthly sales in 19X7 on a 60-day delay basis.

Durgan has not experienced a 60-day collection period in the past and is forecasting 47 days in 19X7. A 60-day collection period is being used for this monthly cash budget for two reasons: (1) It is much simpler to project 60 days than 47 days and (2) it is a conservative, worst-case assumption.

Cash outflows. It is assumed that payments to suppliers will equal the cost of goods sold for the prior month. This assures trade payments on a 30-day basis. Interest and general and administrative expenses will be paid in the month incurred.

Long-term debt payments of $20,000 are scheduled for March, June, September, and December. Mark Durgan plans to purchase $70,000 worth of equipment in March, and taxes of $30,000 will be paid in April. Note that Durgan wants a minimum cash balance of $20,000.

Page 114 shows the monthly cash budget, based on these assumptions.

Durgan Electric Co.
19X7
Projected Monthly Income Statement
($000s)

	Jan	Feb	Mar	Apr	May	Jun	Jul	Aug	Sep	Oct	Nov	Dec	Total
Sales	604	712	913	967	1,948	1,948	1,948	1,639	1,048	672	604	430	13,433
Cost of goods sold	459	541	694	735	1,480	1,480	1,480	1,246	797	511	459	327	10,209
Gross Profit	145	171	219	232	468	468	468	393	251	161	145	103	3,224
Depreciation	11	11	11	11	11	11	11	11	11	11	11	11	132
Other operating expense	214	214	214	214	214	214	214	214	214	214	214	214	2,568
Total Operating Expense	225	225	225	225	225	225	225	225	225	225	225	225	2,700
Operating Profit	(80)	(54)	(6)	7	243	243	243	168	26	(64)	(80)	(122)	524
Other income (expense)	(12)	(12)	(12)	(12)	(12)	(12)	(12)	(12)	(12)	(12)	(12)	(12)	(144)
Pretax Profit	(92)	(66)	(18)	(5)	231	231	231	156	14	(76)	(92)	(134)	380
Income tax													(95)
Net Income													285

Durgan Electric Co.
19X7
Projected Monthly Cash Budget
($000s)

Cash Budget	Jan	Feb	Mar	Apr	May	Jun	Jul	Aug	Sep	Oct	Nov	Dec
Beginning Cash Balance	30	20	20	20	20	20	20	20	20	20	20	100
Cash sales												
Accounts receivable collection	465	434	604	712	913	967	1,948	1,948	1,948	1,639	1,048	672
Total Cash Available	495	454	624	732	933	987	1,968	1,968	1,968	1,659	1,068	762
Trade payments	487	459	541	694	735	1,480	1,480	1,480	1,246	797	511	459
General and administrative expense	214	214	214	214	214	214	214	214	214	214	214	214
Interest	12	12	12	12	12	12	12	12	12	12	12	12
Long-term debt payment			20			20			20			20
Equipment purchase			70									
Taxes				30								
Total Disbursements	713	685	857	950	961	1,726	1,706	1,706	1,492	1,023	737	705
Cash Surplus (Deficit)	(218)	(231)	(233)	(218)	(28)	(739)	262	262	476	636	331	67
Minimum cash balance	20	20	20	20	20	20	20	20	20	20	20	
Bank loan required short-term	238	251	253	238	48	759						
Bank loan repaid short-term							242	242	456	616	231	
Ending Cash Balance	20	20	20	20	20	20	20	20	20	20	100	67
Cumulative bank loan, short-term	238	489	742	980	1,028	1,787	1,545	1,303	847	231	0	

You can see that Durgan needs to borrow some money during the year. The cumulative short-term loan reaches a peak of $1,787,000 in June and is paid off by November.

This shortfall in cash flow needs to be covered by a seasonal line of credit, so this forecast is a very important document to show your banker. The required line of credit should be planned for and approved by the bank *before* the year begins, and the monthly cash budget assists the bank in determining what will be required and how and when it will be repaid.

Every month Mark should compare actual results to projections. This will allow him to take corrective action on a timely basis if projections are not being met.

SUMMARY

The short-range financial plan is a critical exercise for any business. Borrowing requirements can vary from month to month, and management must anticipate these needs and make sure they are provided for.

Continually monitoring and adjusting the short-range financial plan is the only way to manage your business proactively. Without this plan, there is no way to determine whether you are on track or not. If you wait until the year is over and the annual financial statements are complete, it will be too late to take proper corrective action.

If your company is not meeting its goals, you need to either revise operations, have a serious talk with your key employees, or revise your plan. You then need to determine the impact of these changes on monthly profitability and cash flow and keep your banker informed of the changes. No one likes to be surprised— especially those who are supplying you credit.

The next chapter describes how to manage your business for maximum profitability.

Chapter Fourteen

Managing for Maximum Profitability

There's an old business proverb that says "If your outflow exceeds your inflow, your upkeep will be your downfall."

No one sets out to lose money. It is not pleasant. All kinds of bad things happen to a business that is not profitable. Why then, do so many businesses lose money and eventually fail? They don't take prompt and decisive action when necessary. This chapter describes how to keep this from happening to your business.

KEYS TO PROFITABILITY

There are four keys to maximizing profitability in your business: focus, knowledge, sacrifice, and commitment.

Focus

You get done what you focus on. It's that simple. If you continually focus on costs, productivity, efficiency, and eliminating waste, you will maximize profitability for any given level of sales.

Focus, however, starts with the big picture. What is your overall strategy? Where are you going? Why? What business are you *really* in? This focus on overall strategy keeps you headed in the right direction and prevents you from drifting off into costly sideshow ventures. Entrepreneurs love to create things. They are full of energy and enthusiasm, and they often start something new at the expense of their business's basic products or services.

There are unlimited opportunities in business for those with energy and creativity, *but you cannot be all things to all people.* If you try it, you will fail. Walk away from some opportunities, no matter how wonderful they appear to be. Focus on the primary strategy of your business and stick with it. Concentrate on one thing— building profitability—and you will accomplish it.

Knowledge

The next key is knowledge. There is no substitute for it. You may not know how to run a business when you first start, but you had better learn, and the faster the better.

Learn about the true keys to profitability in your business. What are they? Labor costs, proper buying strategies, and intelligent pricing are examples of areas that may be critical in your business, but the most important thing for you to know intimately is your actual cost of providing your product or service.

The vast majority of business owners have no idea what their costs are. Oh, they know how much their rent or insurance expense is. That's not too difficult. But how much does it cost to make and sell one widget? How much does it cost to haul 10,000 pounds of freight 2,000 miles? How much does it cost to make and sell a particular bouquet of flowers? Not knowing your costs leads to a herd mentality. Business owners tend to determine price by observing what everyone else is doing. The blind lead the blind, simply chasing volume without regard to profitability, when pricing is not intelligent and informed.

Sacrifice

If you really want to maximize your profits, you will have to make some sacrifices. You will have to sacrifice products or services that do not fit into your strategy, even though they represent tremendous opportunities. You will have to sacrifice family members who aren't carrying their weight. That's right, you may have to *fire* your kid, grandkid, kid-in-law, nephew, or even your spouse. "Family business" has a nice ring to it, but hundreds of thousands of businesses are severely handicapped because some family members are not a chip off the old block but are employed anyway.

You may have to sacrifice employees or even whole branches or divisions. This is hard. Do it anyway if you want to maximize profits. You are not running a charitable operation and you are not in a popularity contest. Your business can and should be profitable. Besides, if you go out of business, all of your employees will be out of work.

Commitment

The most important key to profitability is commitment. You may go to a particular seminar (or even read this book), get all jazzed up about how to operate your business profitably, and go back home filled with good ideas and intentions. But then enthusiasm fades, the phone rings, and the problems of the moment take over. Nothing at all will happen if you lack the commitment to stick with these ideas.

You need to be really committed to making a profit, not just talk about it. You need to focus on and know your costs on a continuous basis. You need to make sacrifices.

OBSTACLES TO PROFITABILITY

Despite the fact that most business owners want to be profitable, there are several obstacles to focusing on maximizing profits. Among them are bad advice, complacency, misplaced optimism, and ego.

Bad Advice

First of all, your trusted advisors often advise you to make as little profit as possible in order to minimize income taxes. The result of this strategy is that you take your eye off the real goal—making money.

There is a difference between tax planning and profit planning, and tax strategies should never drive your business decisions. Besides, under the current tax laws, there is not much you can do along these lines. Your goal should be to maximize profits in your business, and any efforts to the contrary can be a major distraction.

Complacency

Second, when times are really good it is not that difficult to run a successful, profitable business. Complacency sets in. You relax and lose sight of the financial principles that should be employed in the operation of your business. Ironically, success can plant the seeds of failure later on, when times get tough.

Misplaced Optimism

Third, the very quality that is most admirable about business owners, the thing that prompted them to start a business in the first place against overwhelming odds, is a significant obstacle against taking prompt and decisive action to avoid losses.

That quality is unbridled optimism. "Things are a little tough now, but they're going to get better." All you need to do is hang on a little longer, and everything will be all right. Many cling to this thought right into bankruptcy and failure.

Ego

Finally, the energy and enthusiasm that allowed you to be successful in the struggling wonder years works against you in tough times. You established a business that you could build, not tear down. Cutting back is against your basic nature and causes you to feel bad about yourself and your abilities. It is a hard thing to do, and there is a tendency to take it personally. It seems an admission of failure.

These obstacles need to be identified and dealt with in order to maximize profits and avoid losses. The key message of this chapter is that *it is never necessary to lose money.* Read and follow the principles of this chapter carefully and you will be in a position to maximize your profits, no matter what the situation confronting your business.

COST BEHAVIOR PATTERNS

The first step in maximizing the profits in your business is to recognize that you have two types of costs, fixed costs and variable costs. These costs are classified by how they *behave* in relation to sales. Recognizing the cost behavior pattern in your business is critical to maximizing profitability, and to do it you need to answer the following questions:

1. Which costs are fixed?
2. Which costs are variable?
3. What is the relationship between your variable costs and sales?
4. How can you reduce or minimize your fixed costs?
5. How much fixed costs should you have?

Fixed Costs

Fixed costs are those that *do not vary* with sales. They just keep marching along, no matter how much or how little you sell. For example:

Rent.
Depreciation.
Utilities.
Travel and entertainment.
Legal and accounting services.
Dues and subscriptions.
Insurance.
Advertising.
Transportation.
Interest.
Maintenance and repairs.
Leases.

Some of these costs may seem at first glance to be variable. If you run the machines longer because you have more sales, won't you incur more repair costs? If you have more sales, won't you have more debt and therefore more interest? If you advertise more, won't you have more sales, so isn't that cost variable?

Not really. It is important not to confuse the term *variable* with *controllable*. Variable costs are those that are caused by sales, not costs that can be increased or decreased on a discretionary basis. You may run the machines longer, but the overwhelming bulk of your maintenance costs are going to be fixed. You may borrow more if sales go up, but interest is always classified as a fixed cost. Sales do not cause advertising; advertising causes sales.

If you have a question about whether a cost is fixed or variable, consider it fixed. This is a more conservative assumption for calculating break-even sales. Focusing on fixed costs will allow you to maximize profits and avoid losses. This is an important key to maximizing profitability.

Fixed costs should be monitored continuously during good times and bad. Drastic, prompt action to reduce fixed costs must be taken when times get tough. You should not wait to see if times get better. Branches or divisions should be shut down. People should be let go. Every dime of expenditures should be carefully scrutinized. Tear your business down with the same energy you employed to build it up. Do this, and you will probably survive. Hesitate and you may not.

Cutting fixed costs is hard. There isn't a financial consultant alive who doesn't have horror stories about the consequences of a failure to take prompt, decisive action in tough times. What they say when called in to rescue a desperate situation is, "I wish you had called me sooner. All of this could have been avoided."

Salaries are usually the biggest fixed costs that you have, and reducing them means letting people go. These are people you know, respect, and admire. You probably know their families also. You recruited, hired, trained, and molded them into highly effective employees. They may even be related to you. It is difficult to find good people and excruciatingly painful to let them go. Do it anyway. If your business fails because you were too nice to let someone go, then you and all the rest of your employees lose as well.

You should identify and measure your fixed costs at least quarterly, because fixed costs have a tendency to not be fixed at all. They creep up, little by little, especially when times are good and you are not quite so stringent. Every dollar of fixed costs that you do not need is a dollar less of profits. Keep a careful eye on these costs. Make sure that you do not have more than you absolutely need. The result will be maximum profitability.

Variable Costs

Variable costs are those that are *caused by sales*. If you have the sales, you will have the costs. If you don't, you won't. For example:

Commissions.
Bad debts.
Direct labor.
Raw materials.
Products for resale.
Freight.

The key to managing variable costs is to minimize them *in relation to sales*. In other words, you need to determine the relationship of your variable costs to sales, and then keep that relationship (as a percentage of sales) as low as possible.

An example of managing variable costs is to reduce the direct labor involved in a manufacturing process. If you increase manufacturing efficiency by reducing the labor involved, then you reduce the relationship between variable costs and sales. Another example is to take trade discounts, which will reduce product or raw material costs as a percentage of sales.

The relationship of your variable costs to sales is expressed as a percentage, calculated by dividing your variable costs by sales:

$$\frac{\text{Variable costs}}{\text{Sales}} = \text{VC}\%$$

The basic principle of managing variable costs to maximize profitability is to minimize your variable cost percentage (VC%).

Your job is to constantly dream up different ways to do things. Never defend a method because "That's the way we've always done it." Continually look at your procedures from a fresh perspective. Challenge your employees to operate more efficiently. Ask them how you could do things better. Listen to what they say. Never dismiss an idea out of hand, no matter how silly it may sound.

Change is the only constant you have in business today. Make it work for you to minimize your variable cost percentage.

COST BEHAVIOR ANALYSIS

Once you have determined the variable and fixed costs in your business, analyze this information to answer several important questions.

1. How much do I need in sales to just break even?
   To answer this question, follow these four steps:
   - Determine the dollar amount of your fixed and variable costs. Take your last annual income statement and separate your costs into fixed and variable according to our definitions.
   - Divide your variable costs by the sales for that period to determine your variable cost percentage.
   - Subtract your variable cost percentage (VC%) from 100 percent to determine your contribution margin percentage (CM%), as follows:

$$\begin{array}{r} 100\% \\ -\ VC\% \\ \hline CM\% \end{array}$$

   - Divide your contribution margin percentage into your fixed costs.

$$\text{Break-even sales} = \frac{\text{Fixed costs}}{\text{CM}\%}$$

2. How much in sales do I need to make a certain profit?
   Answer this question by adding your desired profit to the amount of your fixed costs and dividing the total by your contribution margin percentage.

$$\text{Sales} = \frac{\text{Fixed costs} + \text{Profit}}{\text{CM}\%}$$

3. How much additional sales do I need to make the same profit if fixed costs increase?
   Add the increase to your existing fixed costs and then divide by your contribution margin percentage.

$$\text{Sales} = \frac{\text{Fixed costs} + \text{Increase} + \text{Profit}}{\text{CM\%}}$$

4. How much do I need to cut fixed costs if my sales drop below the break-even level?
   Multiply your sales by your contribution margin percentage. This is the maximum fixed cost that you can have and not lose money.

   Maximum fixed costs = Sales × CM%

   Subtract that total from your current fixed costs for the amount that fixed costs must be reduced.

   Current fixed costs
   − Maximum fixed costs

   Reduction needed

5. How many widgets do I need to sell to break even?
   Divide your fixed costs by the unit contribution margin (the price per widget minus the variable cost per widget).

$$\text{Unit break-even} = \frac{\text{Fixed costs}}{\text{Unit contribution margin}}$$

There are probably other questions you can answer by analyzing the cost behavior pattern of your business. Use your imagination. Dream up your own. Become intimately familiar with the way costs behave in your business, and you will be well on your way toward maximizing your profitability.

COST BEHAVIOR STRATEGY

To a certain extent, you can control whether a cost is fixed or variable. Rent, as an example, can be fixed or determined as a percentage of sales (variable). Salespeople can be paid a salary (fixed), or a commission based on sales (variable), or some combination of the two (fixed and variable). Certain manufacturing or professional services can be either subcontracted to others (variable), or done in-house (fixed).

Fixed or variable—which is better? The answer depends on how much risk you want to take. The higher the fixed costs, the higher the risk and the higher the potential profit. The following diagram shows a company with high fixed and low variable costs.

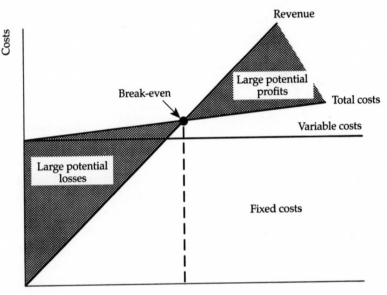

A mix of high fixed costs and low variable costs produces a high break-even sales level and therefore represents a higher degree of risk. The potential profits, however, are very large. Once you pass break-even sales in a business like this, your rewards are great. High risk, high potential reward. Most manufacturing firms are in this category.

The diagram on the next page shows a company with low fixed and high variable costs.

A mix of low fixed costs and high variable costs produces a lower break-even sales level and therefore represents lower risk. The potential profits, however, are much smaller. Once you pass

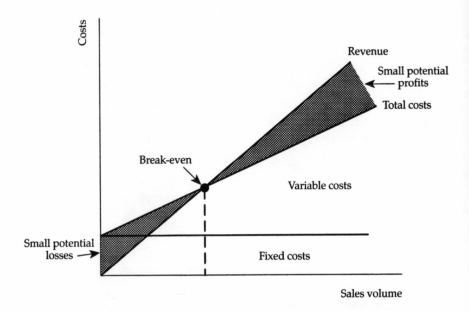

break-even sales in a business with this cost structure, you have to increase sales substantially to make a lot of money. Low risk, low potential reward. Most service firms are in this category.

Study these diagrams carefully. How you position your cost structure will determine how profitable you are for any given level of sales.

If you have little control over your cost structure, then you need to be especially aware of its impact on your risk level and your potential profitability. There may be some steps you can take to mitigate the risk, especially in the start-up phase of business, when risk is already fairly high.

CASE STUDY: DURGAN ELECTRIC CO.

New let's apply cost behavior analysis to the case study.

1. How much in sales are necessary to break even?
   First, classify costs into two groups, fixed and variable. The next page shows the 19X3 income statement for Durgan Electric. In this company, cost of goods sold and bad

Durgan Electric Co.
Income Statement
($000s)

	19X3		Cost
Sales	$4,845	100.0%	
Cost of goods sold	3,755	77.5	variable
Gross Profit	1,090	22.5	
Operating Expense			
Advertising	12	0.3	fixed
Bad debts	48	1.0	variable
Depreciation	53	1.1	fixed
Equipment leases	18	0.4	fixed
Insurance	59	1.2	fixed
Legal and accounting	26	0.5	fixed
Miscellaneous	4	0.1	fixed
Office supplies	25	0.5	fixed
Rent	60	1.2	fixed
Repairs and maintenance	30	0.6	fixed
Salaries, owner	75	1.6	fixed
Salaries, other	459	9.5	fixed
Salary-related expense	88	1.8	fixed
Taxes and licenses	22	0.5	fixed
Telephone	18	0.4	fixed
Travel and entertainment	6	0.1	fixed
Vehicle expense	23	0.5	fixed
Total Operating Expense	1,026	21.2	
Operating Profit	$ 64	1.3	
Interest expense	(10)	(0.2)	fixed
Pretax Profit	$ 54	1.1	
Income tax	(13)	(0.3)	
Net Income	$ 41	0.8	

debts are considered variable because they are caused by sales. All other expenses are considered fixed. This may or may not be the case with your business. If you have included depreciation in your cost of goods sold, for example, then that part of your cost of goods sold will be fixed.

Fixed Costs	Variable Costs
$1,026,000	$3,755,000
− 48,000	+ 48,000
+ 10,000	$3,803,000
$ 988,000	

Second, determine the variable cost percentage.

$$\frac{\text{Variable costs}}{\text{Sales}} = VC\%$$

$$\frac{\$3,803,000}{\$4,845,000} = 78.5\%$$

Third, determine the contribution margin percentage.

100%
− VC%
CM%

100%
− 78.5%
21.5%

Fourth, divide the fixed costs by the contribution margin percentage.

$$\frac{\text{Fixed costs}}{\text{CM\%}} = \text{Break-even sales}$$

$$\frac{\$988,000}{0.215} = \$4,595,000$$

This means that sales can drop about $250,000 ($4,845,000 − $4,595,000) before the company loses any money. This is an especially important fact to determine if sales are declining, as they are with Durgan as of the end of 19X3.

2. How much in sales would be required to make a profit of $125,000?

$$\frac{\text{Fixed Costs} + \text{Profit}}{\text{CM\%}} = \text{Sales}$$

$$\frac{\$988,000 + \$125,000}{0.215} = \text{Sales}$$

$$\frac{\$1,113,000}{0.215} = \$5,177,000$$

This calculation shows that in order for Durgan to increase profits from $54,000 to $125,000 (a 131 percent increase), sales need to increase from $4,845,000 to $5,177,000 (a 6.8 percent increase). This is pretty good news. However, the company will have to maintain fixed costs at $988,000 for this to work.

3. How much will sales need to increase to maintain the same profitability if fixed costs increase $40,000 (when a new controller is hired)?

$$\frac{\$988,000 + \$40,000 + \$54,000}{0.215} = \text{Sales}$$

$$\frac{\$1,082,000}{0.215} = \$5,033,000$$

This calculation indicates that sales must increase $188,000 ($5,033,000 − $4,845,000) if fixed costs increase $40,000, just to make the same profit of $54,000. In other words, sales must go up almost five times the increase in fixed costs just to stay even ($188,000 ÷ $40,000).

Be sure to do this calculation the next time you want to add to the fixed costs of your business!

4. How much do fixed costs need to be cut if sales decline to $4,000,000?

Sales × CM% = Maximum fixed costs

$4,000,000 × 0.215 = $860,000

$988,000   Existing fixed costs
− 860,000   Maximum fixed costs
―――――――
$128,000   Reduction needed

Fixed costs must be reduced by $128,000 (or 13 percent) if sales decline to $4,000,000. This calculation is at the heart of maximizing profitability or minimizing losses. It is probable that people will have to be let go in order to reduce costs that much. Difficult, but necessary.

5. How many light sockets need to be sold to break even?

If Durgan's only product were light sockets, it would be possible to calculate how many must be sold to break even. The calculations are as follows.

$$\text{Break-even units} = \frac{\text{Fixed costs}}{\text{Price per unit} - \text{VC per unit}}$$

$$\text{Break-even light sockets} = \frac{\$988,000}{\$9.00 - \$7.00}$$

$$= \frac{\$988,000}{\$2.00}$$

$$= 494,000$$

This seems like a lot of light sockets, but this example was just made up to illustrate the procedure. Durgan actually sells a variety of electrical products, so this type of calculation does not directly apply to it. If Durgan had a separate division that sold only light sockets, it would be possible to determine the break-even unit level for that division. It would be tricky to allocate the proper amount of fixed costs to that division, but it could be done.

SUMMARY

Maximizing profits or minimizing losses is a function of following several key strategies:

• Make sure your fixed costs are as low as possible for any given level of sales.

- Make sure your variable cost percentage is as low as possible.
- Make every effort to increase sales for any given level of fixed costs.
- Raise prices where possible to maximize your contribution margin percentage.

Downsizing, streamlining, right sizing—these terms are prominent in the 90s. Today's business managers are finding new and creative ways to cut fixed costs. In the global economy in which U.S. companies must operate, competitive pressures simply do not allow for fat or unnecessary expenses. Look carefully around your company. Turn over every rock. See what you can find to save money. Don't just do this once; do it frequently.

If the sales in your business start to decline, you need to take prompt and decisive action. The nature of the action should be planned well in advance. What fixed costs are you going to cut? Who are you going to let go? When are you going to do it?

Remember that it is never necessary to lose money. Losses (other than one-time catastrophes) are a result of a failure to cut fixed costs on a timely basis. This should be fairly comforting: You never have to lose money. Profits or losses, it's up to you. The message of this chapter is that losses are always avoidable and profits are always possible.

The next chapter describes how to analyze the desirability of purchasing additional fixed assets.

Chapter Fifteen

Fixed Asset
Acquisitions Analysis

Y ou will probably need to purchase equipment or other types of fixed assets in your business from time to time. The goal should be to make sure that fixed asset additions are financially sound.

That sounds fairly obvious. Why would anyone buy equipment on anything but a financially sound basis? The fact is, it's done all the time. Analyzing fixed asset acquisitions is difficult to do with any precision, and the method employs concepts that have a textbook ring to them. Besides, business owners tend to believe they have fairly good intuition, and if your gut tells you it's right, it probably is. All those calculations only waste precious time.

Acquiring fixed assets is often more emotional than rational. All your friends at the convention are bragging about their new $100,000 computer system. You are embarrassed to admit that you are still operating with a quill pen and hand-crank calculator, so you vow to buy the same system as soon as you get home.

The latest fax machine can operate directly from your personal computer at home or at the office, on plain paper, in brilliant color. It doubles as a copy machine, makes great espresso, and automatically calls home when you are going to be late. You simply have to have it.

The latest model truck has an eight-speaker stereo system, dual air bags, antilock brakes, all-wheel drive, and a turbo-charged V-8 engine that tops-out at 130 miles per hour. It's available in candy apple red and has room for your toolbox behind the seat. You just have to have it.

You get the idea. These types of decisions are often made on gut instinct or emotions. Rarely is a serious effort made to determine the financial return on the investment. One of the main reasons for this lack of analysis is that it can be complicated and confusing. It appears way too theoretical—something that large corporations hire a staff of MBAs to do, but not at all practical for a closely held business.

ANALYZING FIXED ASSET PURCHASES

It does not have to be this way. Taken one step at a time, analyzing the purchase of fixed assets is a fairly easy process. There are basically four questions to answer as a part of this analysis.

1. How much increased income or decreased expenses can be expected as a result of the acquisition?

   The purchase of a fixed asset should result in either increased income or reduced expenses. If this is not the case, then cash is drained or debt increased without any benefit. The only exception to this is the replacement of something that has broken or worn out. An exhaustive analysis is not necessary if a business has one truck and needs to replace it. It is the purchase of a second truck that needs to be analyzed carefully.

   The savings should be expressed in the form of increased cash flow after tax over the useful life of the equipment, so that the benefit per year can be determined. A second truck, for example, should generate additional revenues. However, there will also be expenses involved in operating the truck, and one of those expenses—depreciation—is not a *cash* expense.

   It is the *net cash inflow* (cash inflow minus cash outflow) that needs to be determined. This may be a level amount per year over the estimated useful life of the truck, or it may vary from year to year. Of course, it will be difficult to pinpoint this over the life of a truck that may last ten years. This is not an exact science, but your best guess is better than nothing.

2. What is the salvage value of the fixed asset at the end of its useful life?

This may be difficult to estimate, but it can sometimes be expressed as a percentage of the initial cost. Or historical experience may assist in this process.

Many items of equipment have an established market, and you can observe what percentage of the original cost is retained in the form of market value. Zero salvage value—say, for obsolete computers—is a conservative estimate to make in the absence of more precise information.

3. What is the useful life of the fixed asset?

   This may also be difficult to determine with precision, but some estimate must be made. There are experience factors for almost every type of fixed asset, and the period allowed by the IRS for depreciation of the asset may be a starting place. Remember that some assets (like computers) are obsolete well before they are worn out.

4. What is the minimum rate of return required on the investment in the fixed asset?

   Return on investment is a concept that has already been discussed in this book. Business owners have a certain amount of money invested in their business and should expect to earn a satisfactory return on that investment. The same thing is true for every purchase of fixed assets.

   Any investment should generate, or at least have the potential to generate, a reasonable return. How *much* of a return is the question, and you can answer it by looking at alternative investments. If you can make a 5 percent return by investing your money in a bank savings account, then investments in your business should generate a higher return than that. Just how much higher is a matter of judgment, and it is based on your assessment of the risk involved.

With these four questions answered, you can determine if an investment in fixed assets is financially sound or not. Future net cash inflows are compared to the initial cost of the asset. Future inflows should exceed or equal the present cash outflow (cost of the asset). This cannot be done on a dollar for dollar basis, however. You have to wait several years for the future cash inflows, and any time you have to wait for your money, it is not worth as much.

Future cash inflows must be *discounted* to take into the account that you can't get the money right away. A dollar in the future is worth less than a dollar today because you have to wait to receive it (losing investment income in the process). The result is called the *present value* of the future cash inflows.

If the present value of future cash inflows equals or exceeds the initial cost, the desired return on investment is achieved. A present value lower than the initial cost means an unacceptable rate of return, and the asset should not be purchased.

CASE STUDY: DURGAN ELECTRIC CO.

Mark Durgan is thinking of purchasing a new computer system that will more easily produce monthly financial statements and computerize the inventory control process. This system will cost $70,000, and he wants to determine the financial desirability of this acquisition.

1. How much can be expected in increased income?

   One person can probably be eliminated due to the efficiencies of this new system. After-tax cash savings are estimated to be $18,000 per year.

2. What is the salvage value?

   The salvage value is estimated to be approximately 10 percent of the initial cost, or $7,000.

3. What is the useful life of this system?

   Estimated useful life of the system is six years.

4. What is the minimum required rate of return?

   Mark has determined that any investment in fixed assets should bring at least a 15 percent after-tax return.

We can use this information to determine whether this investment is financially sound. This is done by determining the present value of the future cash inflows over the life of the asset, using the 15 percent present value factors. The present value of future cash inflows is then compared to the initial cost of $70,000.

If the present value of the future cash inflows is equal to or greater than the initial cost, the investment meets or exceeds the

15 percent return on investment requirement. If the present value of the future cash inflows is less than the initial cost, it will not generate the required 15 percent return.

The next page contains a table that lists the present value factors for returns ranging from 8 percent to 25 percent. The 15 percent factors should be used in this example.

The calculations for Durgan's computer system follow:

Year	Cash Inflow	×	15% Present Value Factor	=	Present Value
1	$18,000	×	0.870	=	$15,660
2	18,000	×	0.756	=	13,608
3	18,000	×	0.658	=	11,844
4	18,000	×	0.572	=	10,296
5	18,000	×	0.497	=	8,946
6	25,000[1]	×	0.432	=	10,800

Total Present Value $71,154

[1]Includes $7,000 salvage value.

The fact that the total present value is *greater* than the initial cost ($71,154 versus $70,000) indicates that the return on this investment is greater than 15 percent. If the total present value were exactly $70,000, the return on investment would be exactly 15 percent. If it were less than $70,000, the return would be less than 15 percent and the investment should not be made.

In this case, a uniform savings of $18,000 per year was assumed over the estimated life of the equipment. This may not always be the case. There may be greater savings in the earlier years, for example, due to increased maintenance in the later years.

With this format and the appropriate present value table, you can perform this type of analysis for any fixed asset acquisition.

SUMMARY

Acquisition of fixed assets requires committing a large portion of your company's resources for an extended period of time. These decisions deserve to be analyzed as carefully as possible. If they

Present Value Factors

				Required Return on Investment					
Year	8%	10%	12%	14%	15%	16%	18%	20%	22%
1	.926	.909	.893	.877	.870	.862	.847	.833	.820
2	.857	.826	.797	.769	.756	.743	.718	.694	.672
3	.794	.751	.712	.675	.658	.641	.609	.579	.551
4	.735	.683	.636	.592	.572	.552	.516	.482	.451
5	.681	.621	.567	.519	.497	.476	.437	.402	.370
6	.630	.564	.507	.456	.432	.410	.370	.335	.303
7	.583	.513	.452	.400	.376	.354	.314	.279	.249
8	.540	.467	.404	.351	.327	.305	.266	.233	.204
9	.500	.424	.361	.308	.284	.263	.225	.194	.16/
10	.463	.386	.322	.270	.247	.227	.191	.162	.137
11	.429	.350	.287	.237	.215	.195	.162	.135	.112
12	.397	.319	.257	.208	.187	.168	.137	.112	.092
13	.368	.290	.229	.182	.163	.145	.116	.093	.075
14	.340	.263	.205	.160	.141	.125	.099	.078	.062
15	.315	.239	.183	.140	.123	.108	.084	.065	.051
16	.292	.218	.163	.123	.107	.093	.071	.054	.042
17	.270	.198	.146	.108	.093	.080	.060	.045	.034
18	.250	.180	.130	.095	.081	.069	.051	.038	.028
19	.232	.164	.116	.083	.070	.060	.043	.031	.023
20	.215	.149	.104	.073	.061	.051	.037	.026	.019
21	.199	.135	.093	.064	.053	.044	.031	.022	.015
22	.184	.123	.083	.056	.046	.038	.026	.018	.013
23	.170	.112	.074	.049	.040	.033	.022	.015	.010
24	.158	.102	.066	.043	.036	.028	.019	.013	.008
25	.146	.092	.059	.038	.030	.024	.016	.010	.007

are made unwisely, they can be difficult or even impossible to reverse.

The hard part of this exercise is not the actual calculations. That is simple arithmetic. The hard part is estimating the future cash inflows and the terminal salvage value of the asset. Always keep in mind that this is not meant to be scientific; no one can predict the future with certainty. But any well-thought-out estimate is better than no estimate at all. Be conservative. Be tough. Be demanding. This is your money, and you should earn a satisfactory return on your investments.

Continually using your emotions as a guide and investing in fixed assets that do not generate a satisfactory return on investment will eventually drag down the entire business. If this happens, you may be better off selling the business and investing your money in something that will provide a higher return.

Don't let your emotions control this decision. Analyze fixed asset acquisitions whether you want to or not. If you are not entirely sure how or why this works, *do it anyway*. Give it your best shot. Anything is better than nothing, and you will gain understanding as you go along.

This analysis is an important tool to help you maximize profits. It will help you build the return on investment in your business and ease you ever closer to the thunder phase.

The next chapter describes how to provide and plan for the financing of your business and discusses some important aspects of dealing with your bank.

Chapter Sixteen

Dealing with Your Banker

M any business owners feel that the only time you can get a loan from a bank is when you don't need it. Some say the only person who hasn't been turned down by a bank is the one who hasn't applied.

Bankers can be difficult. They ask a lot of questions. "Where are you going? How are you going to get there? What does your projected cash flow look like? What is your background and expertise?" By the time you get through with this third degree, you are convinced that bankers were put on earth primarily to complicate your life.

It doesn't have to be that way. Through the proper application of this book, your relationship with the bank will soar to new heights. You will look forward to each visit with your banker. Well . . . maybe that's a little strong. However, doing your financial homework and following the principles of this chapter *will* ensure that your banker becomes an integral and welcome member of your team.

Communication is paramount in establishing a good relationship with your banker, and effective financial management is the key. When you have completed your historical analysis and financial plan, you will gain important credibility as someone who actually has a grasp of his or her business from a financial standpoint. You will stand out as one of a small minority of the bank's customers who routinely provide such information. As the banker gains confidence in your ability to manage the business on a sound financial basis, both you and your banker will be working in harmony for your financial success.

DEBT VERSUS EQUITY

The two sources that are available to provide funds for your business are debt (money from banks, trade creditors, and other lenders) and equity (money from owners). The general rule for financing a business is "Equity first, debt second," because a strong equity base allows you to deal from a position of strength when you seek debt. You will not be as risky, and debt will therefore not be as expensive (in the form of high interest rates) or difficult to obtain.

The reverse is also true. If you reach your borrowing limits and then seek equity capital out of desperation, you will have to give up much more in the way of ownership in order to raise the needed funds. Because your company is risky, equity will be both difficult to obtain and very expensive.

Equity Financing

Equity first, debt second. It sounds simple enough, but it may not always be possible. Where are you going to get equity capital? A full discussion of venture capital or public offerings is beyond the scope of this book, but it is safe to say that few businesses qualify for either. That means that you are probably limited to either raising money yourself (from, say, available savings or the sale or mortgage of your house) or calling on friends and relatives.

If you have already put all of your available funds into the business, then your options are limited to friends and relatives. In fact, your options are probably limited to *older* friends and relatives who have lived long enough to accumulate the money. Your business, however, is not exactly where they ought to be investing their retirement funds. This is a time for them to be taking less risk, not more.

While equity financing is tough, a minimum amount is needed to ensure continued financial viability. Projections of both income statements and balance sheets, as discussed in chapters 10 and 11, will show how much capital is likely to be required. These projections should be updated frequently as new information regarding actual performance becomes available.

If you need to raise equity capital, be sure to seek the advice of qualified lawyers, accountants, and business valuation experts who are experienced in this type of transaction. The legal requirements are complicated, and this should not be a do-it-yourself project. *If you are seeking equity capital, prepare a detailed business plan*, as outlined in the next chapter.

Debt Financing

The discussion of debt financing in this chapter assumes that a commercial bank is the source of the funds. The general principles will apply, however, to other sources of debt, such as business factors, finance companies, savings and loans, insurance companies, and the government.

You are urged to research other available publications for more detailed information if bank financing is not available to you. The Small Business Administration has an extensive list of publications that provide information about financing sources and available programs.

STRUCTURING DEBT

Three main categories of debt are likely to be required in your business: short-term, intermediate-term, and long-term debt.

All of your loan requests are going to fall into one of these three categories, and it is important for you to understand the type of debt you are requesting from the bank. This involves answering two questions:

1. How much are you going to need?
2. How long will you need it?

You would be amazed at the number of business owners who cannot answer those two questions with any degree of accuracy or sophistication. They rely instead on instincts and a seat of the pants approach to financing their business. Then, when they don't get a warm reception at the bank, they complain that bankers aren't there to help at all, but simply to tell them why they can't do something. If they never see the light, these business owners usually become part of the 85 percent that don't survive.

The following diagram illustrates the behavior of assets in your business and how these assets should be financed:

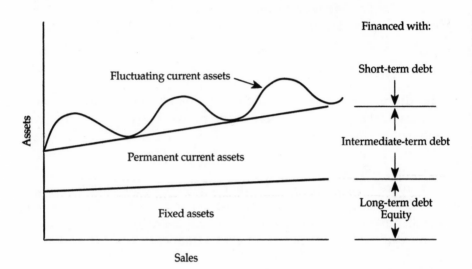

Fluctuating current assets are accounts receivable and inventory that go up or down during the year based on seasonal sales patterns. These assets are financed on a short-term basis.

Permanent current assets represent the minimum level of accounts receivable and inventory required in your business at any time during the year. This level will increase each year as sales increase. Permanent current assets are generally financed with intermediate-term debt.

Fixed assets are made up of land, buildings, furniture, fixtures, and equipment. They are financed with long-term debt and equity.

Short-Term Debt

Short-term debt is debt that is due within one year. It can take the form of a fixed maturity loan, such as 90 or 120 days, or it can be structured as a seasonal line of credit. A seasonal line of credit is negotiated at the beginning of the year and made available as needed during the year. It is used to finance fluctuating current assets.

The seasonal line of credit is expected to start out at zero at the beginning of the year, rise to some forecasted level during the year when fluctuating current assets reach their peak, and fall to zero by the end of the year. If the line of credit does *not* fall to zero by the end of the year, then the debt has moved into the intermediate-term category. The monthly cash budget is the tool to forecast the amount of short-term debt (in the form of a seasonal line of credit) that is required, if any.

If your business is not seasonal in nature, you may still require a short-term loan. You may, for example, have a large insurance premium that must be paid at the beginning of the year. If you do not have the cash available for this expense, then a possible solution is to negotiate a short-term loan that will allow you to make one or more payments during the year as cash flow is available.

Collateral for short-term loans is primarily accounts receivable. Occasionally the bank will lend money on inventory or work in progress, but it is not common and will not be viewed with much enthusiasm. The reason is simple. Inventory is a lot harder to use to pay off a loan than accounts receivable. Exceptions to this are businesses like automobile and appliance dealers that can finance their inventory on a 100 percent basis (referred to as a flooring line of credit).

The bank will require varying degrees of control if accounts receivable are used as collateral. Control can range anywhere from requiring customers to pay the bank directly (referred to as specific notification) to simply monitoring the situation on a monthly or quarterly basis. As a general rule, you can expect the bank to set a loan limit of 70 to 80 percent of your accounts receivable that are under 90 days in maturity. This theoretically gives the bank a cushion in case it has to call the loan and collect the receivables directly for payment.

If your business is not in a position to borrow money from a bank, you may want to explore the possibility of *factoring* your accounts receivable, which involves actually selling your receivables to another party in exchange for cash. As you might guess, factoring is going to be more expensive than borrowing from a bank. The reason for this is twofold: (1) Your business is more risky since you have not qualified for a bank loan and (2) the factoring company usually gets its money from a bank and marks it up before passing it along to you. For this reason, factoring should be a last resort, used only when other sources of money are not available.

Intermediate-Term Debt

Intermediate-term debt is much more difficult to understand and forecast than either short- or long-term debt because of its in-between nature. This type of financing is usually needed by a growing company to finance increases in permanent current assets. Intermediate-term debt is often referred to as a working capital loan, a revolving line of credit, or simply a revolver.

The amount and term of this type of debt are difficult to determine with any precision because it is hard to see the future perfectly. This makes it all the more important for the business owner to forecast and monitor this type of debt as carefully as possible.

Chapters 10 and 11 focussed on forecasting techniques that will help determine the amount of intermediate-term debt you are likely to require. Depending on the situation, it is wise to prepare a range of forecasts that provide both the upper and lower limits of debt that may be required.

Once it is determined that intermediate-term debt has reached a peak, it is often converted to a long-term loan with regular payments, usually with a maturity of five years or less.

Intermediate-term debt is tricky to negotiate because it is basically debt that has no stated repayment schedule and no set maturity (even though it is typically carried on the balance sheet as a 90-day or demand note). Requiring payments on this type of debt would be somewhat fruitless, because the business may need additional debt each year and therefore would not be in a position to make any payments. For this reason, both the borrower and the lender must have a thorough understanding of exactly what is required and when repayment may be possible.

Intermediate-term loans are governed by a loan agreement that spells out the amount of money that will be made available, the time frame that will be used for future review and renewal of the revolving line of credit, and the financial constraints required by the bank (limit on owner's salary, dividends, balance sheet strength, and the like).

Collateral for a revolving line of credit is usually based on a percentage of eligible current assets (80 percent of accounts receivable and 50 percent of inventory), but it is not unusual for the bank to take a lien on fixed assets as well.

Long-Term Debt

Long-term debt is used to purchase fixed assets. The amount of the loan is limited to a percentage of the cost or value of the asset. The term is usually three to seven years, depending on the asset. Land and buildings can typically be financed up to 15 years. Regular payments are required, and interest can be either fixed or floating. Collateral consists of the asset purchased.

Even though the terms of long-term loans are straightforward, banks are often not eager to make them. The reason is that the banker has to make determine the borrower's ability to repay several years down the road, which presents a higher degree of uncertainty and risk. Long-term loans are available only to established businesses with a good payment record and a demonstrated track record of profitability.

Leasing fixed assets is a reasonable alternative to buying, and sometimes the credit requirements are less strict.

LOAN AGREEMENTS

Most loans are covered by some sort of loan agreement, and you can expect to negotiate loan covenants as part of this agreement. Covenants may take the form of a minimum current ratio, a maximum debt to equity ratio, or a minimum dollar amount of working capital or equity. There also may be restrictions on owner's compensation, dividends, and repayment of shareholder loans.

These covenants are negotiable, and you should be cautious about agreeing to standards that you are not confident of achieving. If you fail to comply with any of the covenants, the bank can demand immediate repayment of the balance of the loan—which usually has disastrous effects on the business.

You should also be very cautious about tying up all of your assets for a particular loan, restricting your ability to finance your business in the future. Tying up accounts receivable as collateral for an equipment loan, as an example, would make it difficult or impossible to obtain a seasonal line of credit. Lenders have a tendency to ask for things like this, and you should be firm in resisting such requests.

INTEREST RATES

How, you ask, does the bank determine your interest rate? On some sort of arbitrary, capricious basis? The factors that determine the interest rate you will pay at the bank are these:

1. The risk level of your business.
2. The cost of funds to the bank (interest on certificates of deposit, savings accounts, etc.).
3. The term of the loan. (Longer-term loans are usually riskier and therefore have a higher interest rate.)
4. The amount of the loan. (Smaller loans cost as much to make as bigger loans and therefore may have a higher interest rate.)
5. The collateral. (Some forms of collateral are more difficult and therefore more costly to administer.)
6. The average balances that you maintain in your accounts. (The more you maintain, the lower your rate.)
7. The supply of and demand for loanable funds.
8. The competition.

Many factors determine your interest rate, but you should be aware that interest rates are negotiable. Most lending officers have some discretion about the rates that they can charge; speak up if you feel yours is too high.

Do not, however, be tempted to switch banks frequently to get a somewhat lower interest rate. This will not build loyalty between you and the bank and may eventually hurt your ability to obtain debt. If a competing bank is willing to offer you the same type of loan at a lower interest rate, go back to your bank with this information. It's up to your bank to either meet the competition or risk losing your business.

THE FIVE Cs OF CREDIT

At the risk of oversimplifying the lending process, bankers tend to look at a loan request within the context of the five Cs of credit.

1. Character.
2. Capacity.
3. Capital.
4. Collateral.
5. Conditions.

Character

Bankers want to look you in the eye and see an honest, ethical person looking back. They do not want to deal with people of marginal character, no matter how strong the deal. It is the most important criterion they have, and they will check you out as thoroughly as possible to see if your word is good.

Capacity

Once you pass the character test, you need to demonstrate that you have the capacity to repay the loan. You do this by establishing a track record and presenting well-thought-out projections that indicate repayment is probable.

Capital

Every business needs a sufficient base of capital in order to qualify for bank loans. The amount of required capital is a subjective judgment, but it is usually tied to the debt to equity ratio.

Collateral

There is an unwritten rule in banking that you should never make a loan on the basis of available collateral. This is true because collateral will never make a bad loan good. There should be every indication that the collateral will never be required and is only taken to allow the bank to recover its funds in case of some unlikely problem.

Bankers will always ask for available collateral, but it is no higher than fourth in the order of importance when they decide whether to make a loan. Strong, well-run, and financially stable businesses with a good track record can often borrow on an unsecured basis. You should aspire to reach this point since unsecured, less risky loans are usually granted at lower interest rates.

If you feel that you should be able to borrow on an unsecured basis, sell your case to your bank. If it refuses, shop around. Another bank may see it differently. If so, always give your bank one more shot at it. This courtesy will allow it to decide whether to retain your business on an unsecured basis or let you go to the competition.

Conditions

The last C refers to those conditions that are largely outside your control. What is the condition of the economy? What about your industry? What conditions might impede your ability to repay? How likely are they to occur? Again, this is a judgment call, but it is an important part of the bank's analysis of your credit request.

PERSONAL GUARANTEES

As you have probably already discovered, bankers are trained to look for not one, not two, but *three* sources of repayment. The first (and by far the most desirable) is the cash flow of the business. The second is collateral, and the third is your personal guarantee.

The standard assumption is that bankers never lend to a closely held business without the owner's personal guarantee. This is not true at all. Many businesses are strong enough to stand on their own without the personal guarantee of the owner. If you believe you are in this elite group, then speak up. Make your case. If the bank disagrees, let it tell you why you do not qualify. You can be fairly certain the bank will not initiate the subject of dropping your personal guarantee. If it already has your guarantee, it will want to keep it. If you want to change this situation, it is up to you to bring it up. If you are making a loan request for the first time, state at the outset that you do not expect to guarantee the loan. Test the waters. Your proclamation may be enough to avoid this requirement.

In the final analysis, do not completely rule out a personal guarantee of the loan. This would suggest to the bank that you lack confidence in the ability of the business to repay the loan. Personal liability is something you obviously want to avoid, but not at the expense of restricting the borrowing ability of your business.

RULES OF BEHAVIOR

There are a few rules of behavior that will help you build a good relationship with your bank.

1. Work on establishing a good relationship.

   Invite your bankers to functions of a social, nonbusiness nature. Take them out on your boat, to the football game, or to the theater. Get to know them on more than a business basis in order to deepen your relationship.

   Refer other prospective customers to them. Nothing will cement your relationship like getting them additional business. Make sure your bankers visit your business. Get them on your turf. Let them see the business in action and have them meet your key people.

   Get to know your bankers' boss and maybe even the boss's boss. This will ensure some continuity when they change the lending officer handling your account. (Do not complain about this. It's inevitable, so just make the best of it.)

2. Always be prepared.

   Do not go into your bank with a financial statement penciled on the back of a grease-stained envelope. Imagine that you are the banker. What information would you want? What questions would you have? Anticipate the questions in advance, and be prepared with answers. Never assume that your banker understands your business.

Check the business plan outline at the end of chapter 17 and make sure you have all the information available. Have someone whose opinion you respect review it. Overkill with paper is the key here. Make sure your loan request passes the weight test. More is better. It will make a very good first impression.

3. Keep your banker informed.

   Provide accurate and timely information about your business. Tell it all, the good and the bad. The bank will find it all out anyway, and trying to hide something will hurt your credibility and your relationship.

4. Never bluff.

   If you don't know the answer to a question, say so. If you don't understand something the banker says, say so. Bankers do not mean to be intimidating, and they welcome any questions you have. Don't worry about looking stupid when you ask questions. Bankers have their own jargon, just as you do in your business, and you cannot be expected to be familiar with all of the banking terms. Besides, some banks may define them differently from others. Make sure you really understand what they are saying.

5. Never assume anything.

   Bankers have a way of making statements like "things look pretty good," when they may not mean that at all. It is merely their way of making conversation.

   Bankers want to be liked, just like anyone else, so they often tell you what is really very bad news in a very nice way. When they say you are a special credit, for example, it does not mean they really like you. It means you are one step away from getting booted out of the bank.

6. Never, under any circumstances, surprise your banker.

   This is the most important rule of all. Bankers just do not like surprises. There is a strong temptation to only tell your bankers only what they want to hear or specifically ask about. When they find out the rest of the story, they are surprised. Then they are upset. Then something bad may happen.

SUMMARY

Few things are more crucial to your long-term success than financing your business properly. Analyze your debt requirements thoroughly and communicate this information clearly and concisely to your banker.

Bank debt will either be short-term, intermediate-term, or long-term. Short-term debt (less than one year) is used to finance cash deficits caused by seasonal variations in sales or a specific short-term need, such as paying a lump-sum insurance premium. A seasonal line of credit should be negotiated and set up at the beginning of the year and be completely paid off (cleaned up) by the end of the year. Collateral will be fluctuating current assets (accounts receivable and inventory).

Intermediate-term debt (more than one year but usually less than seven or eight years) is used to finance increases in permanent current assets (minimum levels of accounts receivable and inventory that go up every year due to an increase in sales). This debt is usually governed by a revolving line of credit that is reviewed and renewed every year. While not expected to be repaid within one year, this debt will nevertheless be on a demand type note, and considered to be a current liability by your accountant. Collateral will be accounts receivable and inventory.

Long-term debt (more than one year) is used to finance fixed assets. There is a set maturity, usually five to seven years, and regular monthly or quarterly payments. The amount that is due within 12 months from the date of your balance sheet is considered to be a current liability (current portion of long-term debt), and the balance will be reflected as a long-term liability. Collateral is the fixed asset that is being financed.

Your loans or lines of credit at the bank will usually be governed by a loan agreement which stipulates terms, interest rates, and convenants that restrict your ability to pay dividends, owner's

Alternative Financing Sources

Financing Needs	Financing Structure	Financing Sources
Start-up	Equity	• Wealthy individuals • Venture capital fund • Small Business Investment Co. (SBIC)
Seasonal fluctuations	Short-term debt	• Trade suppliers • Bank • Savings and loan • Commercial finance company • Factoring company • Life insurance company • SBA
Working capital	Intermediate-term debt	• Bank • Savings and loan • SBIC
Fixed assets	Long-term debt	• Commercial finance company • Life insurance company • Leasing company • SBA • Economic Development Administration • Certified or local development company • Factoring company

salary, or shareholder loans. Covenants may consist of a minimum current ratio, a minimum amount of working capital (current assets minus current liabilities), or a maximum debt to equity ratio.

There are six important rules to follow in your dealings with your banker. They are:

1. Establish a good personal relationship.
2. Be prepared.
3. Keep your banker informed.
4. Never bluff.
5. Never assume.
6. Never surprise.

Take great pains to educate your banker about your business and answer any questions that they have. Make sure everyone agrees as to what is expected. Get it in writing. People have a tendency to have selective memories about who said what when problems arise. If you follow these rules of behavior in dealing with those who lend you money, your life will be a lot easier and your reputation as a good businessperson will be greatly enhanced.

The final chapter discusses the overall planning process for your business and where the financial plan fits with the general business plan.

Chapter Seventeen

Putting It All Together

T his book is all about achieving financial success, and the following diagram illustrates the business success process. It starts with strategy formulation, moves to operational planning, and results in financial success.

The Business Success Process

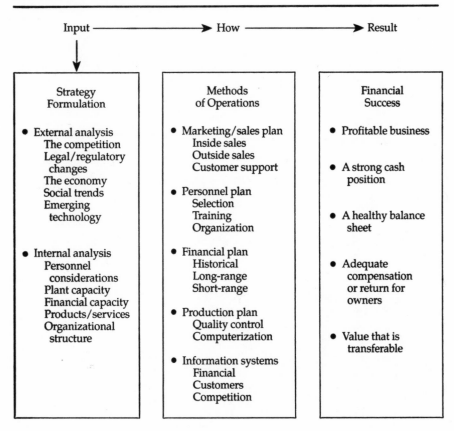

Input ————————➤ How ————————➤ Result

Strategy Formulation	Methods of Operations	Financial Success
• External analysis The competition Legal/regulatory changes The economy Social trends Emerging technology	• Marketing/sales plan Inside sales Outside sales Customer support • Personnel plan Selection Training Organization	• Profitable business • A strong cash position • A healthy balance sheet
• Internal analysis Personnel considerations Plant capacity Financial capacity Products/services Organizational structure	• Financial plan Historical Long-range Short-range • Production plan Quality control Computerization • Information systems Financial Customers Competition	• Adequate compensation or return for owners • Value that is transferable

A detailed outline of what a business plan should contain follows. Examine it carefully. Answer the questions in the checklists for marketing, management, and finance. Become a believer in the planning process. It will pay great dividends in your efforts toward succeeding in your business.

BUSINESS PLAN OUTLINE

I.   Cover Page
    Name of business
    Address and phone number
    Date

II.   Table of Contents

III.   Proposal
    A. Entity seeking funds
    B. Amount needed
    C. Purpose of money
    D. Method and term of repayment
    E. Available collateral and/or guarantors

IV.   Summary
    A. Description of the business
        1. Name and address
        2. Form of business: corporation, partnership, sole proprietor
        3. Founders
        4. Date started
        5. Type of business (manufacturing, retail, wholesale, service, etc.)
        6. Status of business (start-up, expansion, takeover, etc.)
        7. Mission statement
        8. Owners
        9. Key officers/management
       10. Board of directors
       11. Products/services

    12. Area served

    13. Major customers

    14. Method of distribution

    15. Status of industry (growth, decline, maintenance, etc.)

V. Marketing

    A. Description of products/services

        1. Primary benefits

        2. Unique features (style, price, quality, patents, etc.)

        3. Future enhancements

    B. Description of market

        1. Description of customers

           a. geography (location, city size, population density, natural resources, climate, industrial base, etc.)

           b. scope (local, regional, national, international, etc.)

           c. demographic (age, sex, marital status, income, education, etc.)

           d. psychographic (lifestyle, personality, attitudes, etc.)

           e. sociological (religion, race, nationality, social class, etc.)

           f. user behavior (rate of usage, brand loyalty, method of payment)

        2. Size of market (current size, growth potential, concentrations, etc.)

        3. Market status (growing, stable, declining, etc.)

        4. Market share (three-year forecast)

        5. Competition (major competitors [firms and products], market share, strengths, weaknesses, differences, future trends, etc.)

        6. Product comparison (price, performance, durability, speed, size, weight, styling, appearance, ease of operation, etc.)

7. External factors (laws, licenses, customs, trade association, etc.)
8. Marketing strategy
   a. three-year sales forecast (major product lines, existing/prospective customers)
   b. sales strategy (direct, brokers, distributors, franchises, reps, terms)
   c. advertising strategy (budget, method [TV, radio, newspaper, direct mail, word of mouth, etc.])
   d. public relations (publicity, donations, community service, etc.)
9. Pricing strategy
   a. level (skimming, match, over- or undercompetition, etc.)
   b. markups/margins (product, customer group)
   c. discounts (quantity, early payment, etc.)
   d. sales promotions
   e. loss leaders
10. Economic overview
    a. status of economic cycle
    b. impact on the industry
    c. sociological developments
    d. technological developments
    e. seasonality

VI. Management
   A. Principals/key management
      1. Primary duties, work experience, salaries, education, etc.
      2. Organization chart
      3. Directors
      4. Advisors (accounting, legal, insurance, consultants, etc.)
      5. Bank relations
      6. Employees (skills required, wage rates, union affiliations, etc.)

    7. Operations

      a. plant (location, size, special requirements, capacity, condition, expansion plans, lease/rental terms, etc.)

      b. equipment (cost, condition, useful life, etc.)

      c. manufacturing process (in-house, sub, etc.)

    8. Research and development

    9. Areas of concern (high-risk areas and alternative strategies)

VII. Financial

  A. Historical information

    1. Balance sheet spread, five years

    2. Income statement spread, five years

    3. Ratio analysis

    4. Cash flow analysis

  B. Long-range plan (list all pertinent assumptions)

    1. Income statements, three years

    2. Balance sheets, three years

    3. Ratio analysis, three years

    4. Projected cash flow, three years

  C. Short-range plan (list all pertinent assumptions)

    1. Monthly income statements, one year

    2. Monthly cash budget, one year

  D. Capital equipment acquisitions

    1. Equipment needed for three years

  E. Break-even analysis

VIII. Appendix

  A. Principals' résumés

  B. Principals' financial statements

  C. Business and bank references

  D. Job descriptions

  E. Organization chart

  F. Letters of intent

  G. Partnership agreement

H. Buy–sell agreement
I. Leases
J. Contracts
K. Equipment lists
L. Bylaws and articles of incorporation

CHECKLISTS

The three critical areas of any business plan are the marketing, management, and financial sections. Here is where you want to spend your time and do your homework. Following are some of the major issues you should consider as you complete each of these sections.

Marketing

- What exactly are you selling?
- What business are you in?
- Who are your customers?
- Why do your customers buy from you?
- What needs do your products satisfy?
- Who/what is your competition?
- Why/how are you better than your competition?
- What market share do you expect to gain in the next three years?
- What is your advertising and promotion strategy?
- What is happening to your market today? Why?
- How important are your competitors in setting prices?
- What are your competitors' prices?
- What are the costs and gross profit margins of your items by product or service line?
- Does some unique aspect of your product increase its value?
- How does each of the following affect your prices?
Competition.
Supply and demand.

Sales volume.

Business image.

Legal constraints.

- Have you ever asked for an outside evaluation of your products/services?
- How much research have you done about your market and your competitors?

Management

- What is the mission statement of your business?
- What are the major strengths and weaknesses of your business?
- What are your main opportunities and/or threats?
- What are your strategies for exploiting opportunities and avoiding threats?
- What are your strengths and weaknesses as a manager?
- How much management control do you want?
- How many people report directly to you?
- What liability exposures do you have?
- What would happen to your business if you were disabled? If you died?
- What skills do your people need?
- Will you have to train people?
- What licenses and permits are required to operate?
- Do you need to register your trade name?
- Where is your business located? Why?
- What benefits do you expect to offer your employees? Are they competitive?
- What are the risk factors in your business?

Finance

- How much money will you need?
- What do you need the money for?
- When will you need the money?

- How long will you need the money?
- How and when do you expect to repay the loan?
- What do you expect sales and profits to be for the next three years?
- What is your break-even sales level?
- What will your balance sheet look like three years from now?
- What is your expected retum on investment?
- What is the minimum amount of money you need to live on?
- Can your business supply you with your financial needs?
- What is your projected cash flow for the next three years?
- Are your projected ratios in line with industry standards?
- Is your financial performance projected to get better or worse?
- Are your expenses projected to grow faster or slower than sales?
- What are the total start-up costs needed?

The financial plan, as described in this book, is not the only plan you should have. Strategic, marketing, sales, personnel, and production plans are all important in moving toward your goal of financial success. It is not easy work. The first time will be the hardest.

If you faithfully follow the principles of this book, your reward will be arriving at and staying in the thunder phase of business. The chances are excellent that your business will survive you and provide enjoyable employment for many people along the way.

That strikes me as a very satisfying and noble legacy.

Glossary

accounts payable A current liability representing the amount owed to trade creditors for merchandise or services purchased.

accounts payable period (days) The length of time on average it takes to pay trade creditors, calculated by dividing 365 by the accounts payable turnover.

accounts payable turnover The number of times accounts payable turn over per year. This ratio is calculated by dividing cost of goods sold by accounts payable.

accounts receivable A current asset representing money owed for merchandise or services.

accounts receivable collection period (days) The length of time it typically takes to collect outstanding receivables. It is calculated by dividing 365 by the accounts receivable turnover.

accounts receivable turnover The number of times accounts receivable turn over per year. It is calculated by dividing sales by accounts receivable.

accrual basis accounting An accounting system where revenue is recorded when earned and expenses are recorded when incurred, even though cash may not be received or paid out until later.

accrued expenses A current liability representing expenses incurred during a fiscal period but not actually paid by the end of that fiscal period. Examples include interest, salaries, and taxes.

accumulated depreciation The total of all depreciation taken on a fixed asset since it was purchased. Also referred to as allowance or reserve for depreciation.

administrative expenses Rent, utilities, advertising, legal and accounting services, travel and entertainment, and salaries. Also referred to as general and administrative expenses, operating expenses, G&A, indirect expenses, or overhead.

aging accounts receivable Grouping accounts receivable according to the length of time they have been outstanding, for example 0–30 days, 31–60 days, 61–90 days, and over 90 days.

amortization The gradual reduction of a debt by means of equal periodic payments. Also refers to the write-off of intangible assets such as copyrights, patents, or goodwill.

appreciation Increases in the value of an asset in excess of its cost or book value due to economic and other conditions (as distinguished from increases in value due to improvements or additions).

asset Anything owned by an individual or a business that has commercial or exchange value. Assets may consist of specific property or claims against others.

bad debts The amounts due on open accounts that have been deemed to be uncollectable.

balance sheet An itemized statement that lists all of the assets, liabilities, and equity of an individual or business at a given point in time.

balance sheet spread The placing of several years of balance sheets on one piece of paper.

blunder phase The second stage of the business life cycle, also referred to as the high-growth phase.

book value The value of a company's assets, liabilities, and equity as reflected on its balance sheet. Deduct all liabilities from total assets to determine the net book value per share, then divide by the number of common shares outstanding to determine book value per common share. Book value of a company's assets may have little or no relationship to their fair market value.

break-even point The point at which revenues and total costs are equal. A combination of sales and costs that will yield a no-profit, no-loss situation, also known as break-even sales.

budget An itemized listing of all estimated revenue a given business anticipates receiving and the segregation of all estimated costs and expenses that will be incurred in obtaining the income during a given period of time (e.g., a month or a year). Also refers to estimated operations on a cash flow basis (cash budget).

capital The amount of money invested in the business by stockholders. Also referred to as equity and net worth.

capital assets A collective term for all fixed assets of a business, including vehicles, furniture and fixtures, land, buildings, and machinery.

capital budgeting The process of analyzing expenditures for capital (or fixed) assets.

capital gain or loss The difference between the book value and the sale price of a capital asset.

capital stock The shares of a corporation authorized by its articles of incorporation, including preferred and common stock.

cash basis accounting The practice of recording income only when cash is actually received and expenses only when cash is paid out.

cash budget A schedule matching cash inflows against cash outflows over a specified period of time.

cash flow This term may have different meanings depending on who is using it. Bankers usually define it as net profits plus all noncash expenses, but it can also be the difference between cash receipts and disbursement over a specified period of time. As presented by your accountant in the statement of cash flow, it consists of three elements: operating cash flow, investing cash flow, and financing cash flow.

collateral Assets used to secure a loan.

common size balance sheet The process of dividing individual account balances by total assets. Each asset, liability, and equity account is expressed as a percentage of total assets.

common size income statements The process of dividing individual expenses by total sales. Each expense is expressed as a percentage of sales.

contribution margin The difference between sales and variable costs (e.g., $400,000 in sales minus $150,000 in variable costs equals a $250,000 cm).

contribution margin percentage (CM%) The contribution margin expressed as a percentage of sales (e.g., 100 percent in sales minus 37.5 percent variable cost percentage equals a cm of 62.5 percent).

corporation A type of business organization chartered by a state and given legal rights as a separate entity. A C corporation is a taxpaying entity and an S corporation passes its profits (or losses) through to its shareholders.

cost of goods sold Expenses related directly to the production of revenue for a business. This usually includes raw materials, direct labor, freight, and factory overhead for a manufacturing company; merchandise costs for a wholesaler or retailer; and direct labor and materials for a service.

current assets Those assets of a company that are reasonably expected to be converted to cash or consumed within 12 months from the date of the balance sheet. Current assets include cash, accounts receivable, inventories, and prepaid expenses.

current liabilities Liabilities that are due within 12 months of the date of the balance sheet. Current liabilities include notes payable, bank; accounts payable; and accrued expenses.

current ratio A measure of the company's liquidity, or ability to pay its bills, it is calculated by dividing current assets by current liabilities.

debt to equity ratio A measure of the company's safety, or ability to withstand adversity, it is calculated by dividing total liabilities by equity.

depreciation expense The amount of expense a company charges against earnings to write off the cost of fixed assets over their useful life. If the expense is assumed to be incurred in equal amounts in each business period over the life of the asset, the depreciation method used is straight line. If the expense is assumed to be front loaded and incurred in decreasing amounts in each business period over the life of the asset, the method used is said to be accelerated. Frequently, accelerated depreciation is chosen because it is advantageous taxwise to expense deductions as rapidly as possible. Accelerated depreciation is also referred to as declining balance, double declining balance, or sum-of-the-years' digits.

dividend That portion of a corporation's earnings that is paid to the stockholders.

entrepreneur One who assumes the financial risk of the initiation, operation, and management of a business enterprise.

equity The net worth or ownership interest in a company. It is the difference between the assets and the liabilities of a company. In a corporation, equity consists of capital stock, capital surplus, and retained earnings. Also referred to as capital, net worth, and owner's equity.

FIFO (first in, first out) A method of accounting for inventory that assumes the first items received are the first ones sold.

financial impact analysis The process of determining the dollar value of performance deviations. It states in dollars actual compared to expected performance.

fixed assets Assets of a permanent nature, which will not normally be converted into cash during the next 12 months. Examples are furniture and fixtures, land, buildings, and equipment. Also referred to as capital assets.

fixed costs Those costs that do not vary directly with sales. Examples include depreciation, rent (other than percentage rents), and administrative salaries.

fluctuating current assets Those assets that go up and down based on seasonal fluctuations in sales. Typically they are the seasonal demands for inventory, cash, and accounts receivable.

generally accepted accounting principles (GAAP) These principles are established by the Financial Accounting Standards Board (FASB), and all certified public accountants (CPAs) are required to follow them.

goodwill An intangible asset that arises when assets are purchased for more than their fair market value. Generally accepted accounting principles require that goodwill be amortized over a period of four to 40 years.

gross profit The difference between sales and the cost of goods sold.

gross profit ratio The gross profit expressed as a percentage of sales (e.g., 100 percent in sales minus 75 percent cost of goods sold equals 25 percent gross profit).

income statement The statement of sales and expenses for a particular period of time. Also referred to as a period statement.

intangible assets Nonphysical assets such as goodwill, patents, and trademarks.

inventory turnover The number of times a business turns its inventory over during the year.

investing cash flow The cash flow that a company generates based on changes from one year to the next in investments and fixed assets.

leasehold improvements Improvements made to leased facilities that are typically expensed over the remaining period of the lease. Title of leasehold improvements reverts to the landlord at the end of the lease.

liabilities Amounts owed by a person or a business.

LIFO (last in, first out) Method of accounting for inventory that assumes the last item purchased is the first one sold.

line of credit An agreement between a bank and a customer whereby the bank agrees to lend the customer funds up to an agreed maximum amount. A line of credit is widely used for seasonal needs to finance inventory and/or accounts receivable.

liquidity A firm's ability to meet its current obligations.

long-term debt Obligations that are due at least 12 months after the date of the balance sheet.

markup The difference between the cost and the selling price of merchandise. Expressed as a percentage, markup is calculated by dividing the difference between sales price and cost by the cost.

mortgage A long-term debt with real estate or other fixed assets pledged as collateral.

net income The difference between sales and expenses after tax for a fiscal year. Also referred to as net profit after tax and after-tax profit.

net present value (NPV) The present value of future returns, minus the initial cost of the investment.

note payable A written promise to pay certain amounts at certain times.

operating cash flow The cash flow the company generates from operations.

operating expense Those expenses pertaining to the normal operation of the business, excluding interest expense and nonrecurring losses. Also referred to as overhead.

operating profit The difference between gross profit and operating expenses.

permanent current assets The minimum base of current assets (inventory, accounts receivable, and cash) that a business must have on hand at the low point in its seasonal cycle.

plunder phase The last stage of the business life cycle. Also referred to as the decline/renewal stage.

preferred stock Stock that grants its owners certain preference rights over other stockholders on payments of dividends or distribution of assets.

present value The value today of a future payment or stream of payments, after it is discounted at an appropriate discount rate.

pretax profit The difference between operating profit and other income and expense. Also referred to as net profit before tax.

profit plan A projection of sales, expenses, and the resulting profit for the fiscal year.

quick assets Cash, accounts receivable, and marketable securities.

quick ratio The relationship between quick assets and current liabilities, a measure of liquidity.

retained earnings An accumulation of earnings that have been retained over the life of a business and not paid out to stockholders.

return on assets (ROA) The ratio of pretax profit to total assets.

return on equity (ROE) The ratio of pretax profit to equity or net worth. Also referred to as return on investment.

revenue Synonymous with sales; usually used in service businesses.

sales to assets ratio Ratio calculated by dividing sales by total assets.

secured loan A loan secured by some sort of collateral. Secured loans may be either long- or short-term loans.

self-liquidating loan A short-term loan, usually supported by a lien on a given product or commodities, that is liquidated from the proceeds of the sale of the product or commodities.

specific identification A method of accounting for inventory that specifically identifies the particular inventory that was sold versus either LIFO or FIFO accounting for inventory.

stockholder A person owning shares of the capital stock of a corporation. Also referred to as a shareholder.

straight-line depreciation A method of writing off fixed assets at an equal amount per year over their useful life.

sustainable growth rate The maximum amount a business can grow while maintaining the existing debt to equity ratio.

term loan A long-term loan (more than one year).

thunder phase The third stage of the business life cycle, often referred to as the mature or established stage of business.

trend analysis The process of measuring financial data over time to note any significant changes in performance from period to period.

variable costs Costs that are caused by sales. Examples include commissions, direct labor, raw materials, and bad debts.

wonder phase The first phase of the business life cycle, commonly referred to as the start-up phase.

working capital Current assets minus current liabilities.

Index